Praise for C

"*Connect with Your Team* covers 10 skills that make up the most important ingredient in any successful team: effective communication. My favorite sections are about offering encouragement and expressing appreciation—actions I like to call 'catching people doing things right!' Thanks, Denny and Meredith. Because of your book, thousands of teams will communicate at a higher level."

 —Ken Blanchard, coauthor of *The New One Minute Manager®* and
  Leading at a Higher Level

"I love this book. Being in HR for over 30 years, communication is a skill that takes time to master. Building up individuals, teams, and a company takes a ton of good and ongoing communication, years of practice, constant feedback, and the most important skill is listening so you can hear what others need to grow and achieve their goals. I will use this book for all of our new supervisors and for those who want to move into leadership roles. It has a great flow, and the skill chapters can be used in any sequence."

 —Rogene Smith, Director of Human Resources, Conductix-Wampfler

"I've learned that if you focus on communicating well with people, you can have a significant ripple effect on countless others. This book is an amazing how-to guide that everyone can understand and relate to instantly. While I already feel listening is one of my strengths, I read this book to help me become more intentional in all areas of my communication. Clear communication is becoming a lost art amidst a world of texting, emailing, and virtual relationships. Coates and Bell truly have done a wonderful job illuminating a wise, modern-day path for enhancing communication and relationships at work and in daily life."

 —Jonathan Keyser, Founder, Keyser Commercial Real Estate

"To become unshackled, you must have a team. Unfortunately, most team leaders fail unless they have been properly coached. You now hold in your hand the playbook on how to build and coach a superior team."

 —Aaron Scott Young, Chairman at Laughlin Associates, Inc, and
  Founder of The Unshackled Owner

"One of the greatest ways to learn to communicate effectively is by listening and asking questions to better understand who you are communicating with.

I found that *Connect with Your Team* provides excellent insight to being an effective leader. Furthermore, the book details questions and ways to continue communicating that you can begin to implement immediately. I highly recommend this book to support your continued learning on how to communicate more effectively."

> —**Jill Joiner**, MSOD, Leadership Development Specialist, Maine-Health

"*Connect with Your Team* is a beautiful testament to the decades Meredith and Dennis have dedicated to helping leaders and their teams achieve high levels of excellence. If only I had the wisdom contained in this book when I entered my first leadership position 25 years ago, I would have helped more people achieve excellence quicker and in a less painful manner. This duo is a gift to leadership!"

> —**Cynthia Beiler**, President, Leveraged Mind Consulting

"I read *Connect with Your Team* by Denny Coates and Meredith Bell and was blown away by how useful this book is for so many purposes. I've been working with leaders across many industries and sectors for over 40 years, and I wish I had this book back then with the insights and practical tips it offers. It has so much great information that it will serve as a reference book for my practice. I also plan to have my clients read it so they can become even better. Do yourself a favor and read this book several times as you will grow every time you read it. I did...and still do."

> —**Mark Spool**, Ph.D., President, Management Development Solutions

"For the past 20-25 years I have served in the development, oversight and finally as an instructor for the Pennsylvania Child Support Enforcement Training Institute (PACSETI). Our mission is to provide county governmental employees the knowledge and skills to improve performance and enhance the lives of their clients. Prior to *Connect with Your Team,* many of the training materials we reviewed were geared towards corporate America and had limited application for local county government. With Meredith and Denny's book there is finally a training guide well suited for and with practical applications at the local level. I highly recommend it and consider it a must read for any county Director or Team Leader who aspires to improve their skill set and improve their team."

> —**Larry R. Wolfe**, Instructor, Pennsylvania Child Support Enforcement Training Institute (PACSETI) and The Pennsylvania State University Justice and Safety Institute

"Thank you, Meredith and Denny, for bringing your expertise to a wider audience through this book. Our 30 years of working with teams can attest to the fact that the communication skills you identify as the top 10 are right on target. And more importantly, you have described them in a clear, actionable format ready for individual or team development. The concepts of Communication Moments and Communication Mindsets, connected to each skill, make this a book that readers will want to keep by their side and make a part of their daily routine. My advice: Don't just read it; work it!"

—**Rick Stamm**, Founder, The TEAM Approach

"At last—a book that brings it all together. I plan to share this gem with my family, friends and clients. I wish it could be used as essential reading for children and young adults. I truly appreciate the reminder that we must train our brain with constant repetitions, and use these skills everyday as we build new skill memory. It is also noteworthy, that as effective communicators, there is a moment to use these skills in order to be successful. Ignoring the timing of our communication, and pushing our impulsive point of view, leads us into hurt feelings and busted trust. There is something in here for everyone who is in a relationship inside or outside the workspace. In a few years, I envision a well-worn, dog-eared and highlighted copy carried with me as a close companion ready to reference."

—**Alice Dendinger**, SPHR, HR & OD Strategist, Austin Alliance Group

"This book is like a review of Military Leadership Training and traditional education combined into one. The layout makes it an easy read and the inserts are very thought-provoking."

—**Kenneth Mayes**, MBA, Installation Program Manager, Onward to
      Opportunity IVMF at Syracuse University

"With *Connect with Your Team*, Denny and Meredith take the wise counsel I've trusted for nearly 25 years to a whole new level. Their summary of universal leadership communication skills—best case and worst case—along with practical steps to capture moments and implement mindsets, provides a robust resource for anyone ready to raise their leadership game."

—**Janyne Peek Emsick**, Ph.D., Founder, YourExecutiveCoach.com

"Dr. Coates and Meredith Bell have done an exceptional job providing the foundational communication elements to easily connect with your team. This book is a must read for any manager that wants an easy-to-understand approach to deliver communications in a simple, straight-forward manner. The examples are easy to follow with great tips on how to apply the tools to truly make a difference in your workplace. This is an excellent book to help any manager who wants to improve the top 10 communication skills. Buy it and apply it!"

—**Dr. Kevin Gazzara**, Founder and CEO, Magna Leadership Solutions

"Denny Coates and Meredith Bell have put together a well thought out and informative way to raise your communications skills markedly. I especially enjoyed reviewing my knowledge of the Thomas-Kilmann model in conflict resolution where all parties involved can gain a 'win' to a conflict that results in no deterioration of relationships in the workplace. Well done!"

—**Terry Earthwind Nichols**, Author, *Profiling for Profit: What crossed arms don't tell you...* and Chairman, EvolutionaryHealer

"In a nutshell, this is THE *relationship building handbook* for anyone who wants to create positive, productive connections whether you're leading a team and/or nurturing relationships with family and friends. Meredith and Denny combine their wealth of experience, packing this book with the how-to's, whys and benefits behind powerful communication mindsets and skill sets. A must read for any leader who wants to build a high-performing, collaborative team and a culture of mutual caring, trust and respect!"

—**Melissa Ford**, Melissa Ford Coaching and Author, *Living Service: The Journey of a Prosperous Coach*

"I have three observations about the book *Connect with Your Team*. First, this book is born of decades of experience from Denny Coates and Meredith Bell, two people with tremendous knowledge and insights about leadership and coaching. Second, this book is light on theory and heavy on the practical application of important skills—the kind of book I really appreciate. Finally, it's been said that leadership is a conversation. In my experience this is largely true. What is also true is when I was a new leader, I didn't know how to have the important conversations leaders need to have. I learned by trial and error, and error and error. Over the years, I learned to master these critical conversations. The opportunity this book provides is to cut years off mastering the essence of leadership—conversations that help people grow, perform and prosper."

—**Mark Hinderliter**, Ph.D., CPC, Executive Coach

"This book is packed full of wisdom and kindness. I am intellectually smart about lots of things; however, reminding myself to behave in the way that I know is best is a constant challenge. Practicing and being true to these 10 skills will be transformational. You'll learn how to be a better leader and a better person, and you'll be rewarded with richer and deeper relationships."

    —Kristin Hinrichs, Chief Effectiveness Officer, Best in Learning

"I have worked with Meredith and Denny for over 20 years now and at last, here is the book that both summarizes the many golden nuggets of their experience, knowledge and wisdom they have provided to me over those years and encourages me to further my development and become an even better communicator. Regardless of your current skill level/standard of communication, if you read, digest and put into practice the many practical examples and ideas within the pages, you CAN NOT fail in becoming a better, enhanced communicator—no question about it!"

    —Graham Da Costa, Chief Executive, Shine Feedback Ltd

"Denny and Meredith's writing is a fresh perspective on inspirational leadership, achieved by cultivating the vital art form of effective communication."

    —Amy Sargent, Executive Director, Institute for Social and Emotional Intelligence

"In *Connect with Your Team*, Dennis Coates and Meredith Bell present a wealth of highly practical and accessible information based on science, incredibly relevant research, and their own direct and extensive personal experiences. I plan to keep this book close at hand, and fully expect it to be a valuable resource to me both professionally and personally."

    —Steve Peglar, Senior Vice President, The WhitneySmith Company

"As we reinvent a new economy and 'how we work' norms, we all will need to engage in transformational learning. Dennis and Meredith have made another significant contribution to Learning and Development with *Connect with Your Team*. Especially during this period of transition, the book provides the fundamentals to transformational learning at the core levels of communicating. A great contribution to all of us, regardless of our roles at work or personal interactions."

    —David C. Miles, Ed.D., Miles Lehane Companies a Global Leadership firm, prior Marriott Executive

"While this fast-moving book appears to be an 'easy read,' it will become your critical handbook for communication and relationship-building skills. Each chapter provides amazing recipes, consisting of a lesson, prescriptive advice, scenarios, typical questions, tips, and summaries to help you learn and

practice skills that you can use immediately to implement, strengthen, and ingrain practical interpersonal communications skills in your life."
—**Nicholas J. Scalzo**, Ed.D., President, OnTrack Training LLC

"'One cannot not communicate.'—That's the reality! And having this at the top your mind is more important than ever. Thanks, Dennis and Meredith, for this how-to guide to help us develop crucial communication skills to strengthen workplace relationships (even when we are remotely located)."
—**Ana Melikian**, Ph.D., Director of Education for Book Yourself Solid®

"Great leaders are not born, they are developed. Those we see as great leaders have spent many years perfecting the skills that cause us to experience them as influential, persuasive, and inspiring. In *Connect with Your Team*, the authors break down the skills that, when put into practice with intention, can develop any individual into a truly effective leader. This book also addresses the common failure of many books and training—the lack of sustainability. Knowledge is not power; applied knowledge is power. This book will not only teach you the skills but also how to regularly put these skills to use to make a lasting, positive impact on your working relationships. This book should be in the library of any leader who wants the best for their people and organization."
—**Jodi Flynn**, Women Taking the Lead

Connect with Your Team

Other Books by Dennis E. Coates, Ph.D.

For Business

Peer Coaching Made Simple

The Dark Secret of HRD: Four Things You Need to Know to Stop Wasting Money on Training

For Parents

Connect with Your Kid

Parents Coaching Parents

Preparing Your Teen for Life

How Your Teen Can Grow a Smarter Brain

Conversations with the Wise Uncle

Conversations with the Wise Aunt

Other Books by Meredith M. Bell

Peer Coaching Made Simple

Strong for Performance: Create a Coaching Culture with Learning & Development Programs That Stick

Purpose, Passion and Profit (co-author)

Connect with Your Team

Mastering the Top 10 Communication Skills

**Dennis E. Coates, Ph.D.
Meredith M. Bell**

First Summit Publishing

Printed in the United States of America
First Summit Publishing
An imprint of Performance Support Systems, Inc.
757-873-3700

Cover and book design: Paula Schlauch

ISBN: 978-1-7348051-1-6

Quantity sales. Special discounts are available on quantity purchases by corporations, associations and others. For details, contact us at info@growstrongleaders.com or 757-656-4765.

We dedicate this book to the millions of people who have used our assessment and development systems to improve leader and team communication skills. More than any other influence, the experiences and feedback you've shared these past 30 years have shaped our thinking.

Contents

Foreword

I gave my first presentation for a multi-national company as part of a conference on "Innovating to Manage Accelerating Change" in 1979. The company had just completed a global survey of what was known then as "employee satisfaction." What was the number one issue identified by the survey? Yup, "Communication."

Today these surveys focus on what's known as "employee engagement," and although much has changed, "communication" remains the number one issue for people at all levels of all kinds of organizations. It's also the main challenge to happiness in our personal relationships. Of course, "communication" isn't the problem, the problem is *miscommunication.*

Over the years I've met many people who know about miscommunication. Generally, the psychotherapists know more than the managers; but divorce lawyers know more than anyone. An attorney friend who specializes in mediation and "no-fault" divorce mentioned that a woman came into her office recently and proclaimed, *"I want to divorce my husband!"*

The attorney knows the importance of one of the great lessons you'll learn in this book, which is to listen first and then ask questions. So she asked the woman, *"May we start with a few questions?"* Here's the ensuing dialogue:

"Like what?"

"Well, why do you want a divorce? Do you have any grounds?"

"Yes, we have some property, about 5 acres in Westchester."

"No, that's not what I meant. Do you have a grudge?"

"No, but we have a carport right next to the house."

"Hmmm, let me rephrase my question. What are your complaints about your husband?

1

"What do you mean?"

"Well, does he beat you up?"

"No, he gets up at 7 a.m., and I'm usually up an hour before him every day."

Exasperated, the attorney pleads, *"So I don't understand, what's the problem? Why exactly do you want to get a divorce?"*

"Well," she replies, *"he just can't communicate!"*

It's fun to laugh about miscommunication, but it's a serious issue, especially if you lead any kind of team. What are the most important practical skills that we all need in order to build stronger relationships, and how can you cultivate them? Dennis Coates and Meredith Bell bring their compassion, experience and wisdom to identifying these skills, and then coach you to discover the mindset and the methodology for improving them continuously.

And, yes, these skills do require continuous improvement. The 10 essential skills that are the heart of this book are not items that can ever be checked off a list as completed, but rather they form the framework for a lifetime of exploration and growth, both personally and professionally. Just as the best golfers are always working with a coach to improve the key elements of their game, so the best leaders do the same with communication skills. The term "mastering" in the subtitle implies a never-ending process, a growth mindset, and a lifelong quest for sharper interpersonal acuity.

I've been engaged in a lifelong quest to learn and teach creative thinking and to understand and streamline the process of innovation. Creativity and innovation drive human progress. Creative thinking is the skill of generating new ideas that have subjective value; and innovation involves translating those creative ideas into objective value. In *How to Think Like Leonardo da Vinci*, I present history's greatest creative genius as a role model for creative thinking, and in *Innovate Like Edison* (coauthored with Edison's great-great grand-niece Sarah Miller Caldicott) we share the wisdom of history's greatest innovator. My passion for creativity and innovation is undiminished, and over many years of consulting and coaching for companies of all sizes in a wide range of industries, it has become clear to me that teaching people to generate new and valuable ideas is relatively easy. The greatest obstacle to the application of innovative initiatives is miscommunication. So, I've been working to help my clients overcome this challenge and bridge the gap between generating great ideas and applying them successfully. This compelled me to write *The Art of Connection* and *Mastering the Art of Public Speaking,* and to seek out other resources that I can recommend to my clients to help them cultivate better relationships.

Connect with Your Team is at the top of my list. Why? Because Denny and Meredith understand how to weave together the art of learning how to learn with their exceptional expertise in the skills and subskills needed to communicate effectively.

Meredith's book *Strong for Performance: Create a Coaching Culture with Learning & Development Programs That Stick* and Denny's *The Dark Secret of HRD: Four Things You Need to Know to Stop Wasting Money on Training* help us understand how they were able to come together to craft a manual on improving communication skills that won't waste your money or your time, because the lessons will stick with you.

Whatever roles you play in the course of your career or at home, you'll discover that the ability to connect with others effectively is the key to a more creative, innovative and successful life. Tony Award winning actress and comedian Lily Tomlin has played many brilliant roles over the course of her career. One of her classics involved satirizing the miscommunication of telecommunication companies as the obnoxious telephone operator Ernestine who relished asking hapless customers, "Is this the party to whom I am speaking?" Tomlin muses, "I always wanted to be somebody but now I realize I should've been more specific."

Who do you want to be? What are your most important personal and professional goals? As Tomlin suggests, make them specific, articulate your noblest most creative dreams, and then use these 10 priceless skills to make them come true.

Michael J. Gelb
Author, *How to Think Like Leonardo da Vinci* and *The Art of Connection*

Introduction

The executives who run organizations and the leaders who manage the people who get the work done all want the same thing: people consistently delivering high levels of performance and cooperating with each other to achieve team objectives.

And yet, everyone knows this is an elusive goal, because even though people have talents and strengths they can bring to a difficult challenge, you can't simply demand that they give that much to their work. The reality is that if people are to achieve what they're capable of achieving, *they have to want to.*

But all too often, employees are pushed hard to do more by people in positions of authority who don't fully appreciate the challenges or the difficulties workers face. The talented individuals, the ones the organization worked so hard to hire, often feel they don't get the support or respect they deserve. When problems arise, they aren't always listened to. Instead of being consulted to help find solutions, they often find themselves on the receiving end of blame, lectures, commands, and threats—or worse. They also know they don't have to give the kind of performance they're capable of in order to comply with job descriptions and stay employed. The result: unhappy employees sometimes leave the organization in search of a better work environment.

This book is about ways of communicating in the workplace that are based on awareness, appreciation, and compassion. By improving 10 empowering interpersonal communication skills, people can strengthen workplace relationships and inspire each other to do their best. These skills are:

- Listening to understand

- Coaching people to think for themselves

- Guiding learning from experience

- Getting buy-in for expectations
- Offering encouragement
- Expressing appreciation
- Giving feedback constructively
- Accepting feedback graciously
- Engaging in dialogue
- Resolving conflict creatively

To be sure, there are many more interpersonal skills than these ten. However, we've been helping adults acquire these skills for more than 40 years; and from our experience, we've concluded that these are the skills that deliver the greatest impact. Each skill consists of essential elements, or subskills.

Mastering a skill requires that you establish a habit for using it. And to do that, you need to use it repeatedly over time. You may sometimes forget or make mistakes, but you can learn from these shortfalls as you gradually connect the brain cells involved in performing the skill into physical circuits.

During the past 40 years, dozens of books have been written about interpersonal skills, and we list our favorites in Appendix 1 ("Summary of Suggested Reading). They all make a strong case for using skills such as listening, feedback, and conflict resolution. Their main purpose has been to motivate and inspire people to adopt more effective ways of communicating.

Our book has a different purpose. We assume that you already understand the many benefits of connecting more effectively with others where you work; this is why we only briefly talk about "the why" before focusing on the main event: "the how-to." The purpose of our book is to give you clearly stated instructions for applying the skills in the best possible way. Each chapter was written to be a guide and reference as you work on ingraining new behavior patterns.

Because the huge payoffs for communicating effectively (and the consequences for failing to do so) are universal, we wrote this book to be a guide for everyone in the organization: executives, managers, and the people who get the work done. To achieve their potential, everyone needs to improve their communication skills. In the best organizations, talented members of high-performing teams have the capacity to coach each other and lead each other. And some of these individuals will eventually be promoted to formal leadership positions.

As in learning the basic skills of an art form or a sport, becoming proficient with interpersonal skills takes time and effort. You can learn to paint or play golf on your own, but it helps to have a teacher or coach to keep you focused on the fundamentals. Think of this book as your coaching reference.

Part One of this book describes the magnitude of the opportunity. It explains that team members give their best at work if they know, like, and trust each other and their managers; that when issues arise at work, emotional reactions threaten workplace relationships and dampen performance. It goes into detail about how to master a communication skill—or any skill, for that matter.

Part Two is your main coaching reference. Each of the 10 skill chapters follows a similar format:

- What typically happens—and why—when someone fails to use the skill

- Description of the skill

- How to recognize opportunities for using it

- The ideal mindset that empowers success

- Descriptions of the subskills or steps

- Scenarios that illustrate using the skill

- Tips, reminders and encouragements

- Suggestions for further reading

You don't have to read the chapters in sequence; you can choose to start with any of the 10 skills. However, we always advise people to begin practicing listening skills first. To be effective in relationships, you'll need to use listening more often than any other skill, and it's often a component of the other skills. Before attempting to take on the other skills, we recommend that you stick with practicing the elements of listening until they start to feel natural and automatic. As any coach will tell you, to accomplish this *you gotta get your reps.*

Learning to be an effective listener and mastering the nine additional skills will take time. Our advice: *be patient.* It will take lots of workplace application to wire your brain for the skills and achieve the results you seek. Any artist or athlete will tell you that. They'll also tell you that you never get to the end of your mastery; if you're willing to work at it, you can continue to improve for the rest of your life.

We wrote this book to be a companion reference for people who are learning from experience using Strong for Performance, our online app for virtual peer coaching during the extended period of skill reinforcement. The book is also an effective standalone resource when this technology isn't available.

In Part Three, we outline a plan we believe will work to make you a better communicator. Like improving your serve in tennis, learning to hit a golf ball out of a variety of sand traps, or baking a better croissant, becoming the best manager or coworker you can be will be a journey. But it's definitely doable, if you use this book to learn about the skill, commit to applying it in the workplace, work through discouragement, and learn from your mistakes.

And above all: *if you don't give up.*

Denny and Meredith

....

PART ONE

Three Things You Need to Know

As a young man, Denny decided he wanted to play golf. He got the best clubs he could afford and studied the best books about golf. However, on the golf course he learned that there's nothing easy about golf. He realized that there's no substitute for lots of practice, a coach, and the patience to learn from experience.

Like golf, the basic elements of communicating one-on-one effectively are simple. Also like golf, it takes time to replace old habits, which by now are hard-wired in your brain. But if you commit to applying what you learn, you can persist until you master the skills described in this book. Millions of people have done it, and so can you.

To sustain your commitment and feed your success, you can start by appreciating three things:

- If you want people to do their best work, you need to build relationships through effective communication.

- The tendency to lead with authority can get in the way of creating mutually respectful, productive relationships.

- The first step to mastering communication skills is understanding how skill-building works.

"Enthusiasm is the match that lights the candle of achievement."

William Arthur Ward

1

....

They Have to Want To

The literature about leadership, teams, and performance improvement often includes a statement that organizations are made of people. This rather obvious reminder is the foundation principle for any guidance about how to lead more effectively, how to build teams, and how to improve performance.

Except that it's not so obvious. In airports, grocery stores, post offices, and waiting rooms, you'll find yourself surrounded by an incomprehensible variety of people. The next time you drive to one of these places, take a look at the cars coming at you from the opposite direction. Most of the time you perceive them as background activity. Involved in your own thoughts, you probably don't notice the individual drivers or passengers. Even at a stop light, if you happen to glance at the car next to you, you won't be able to see your fellow traveler clearly. Driving at night, all you'll see is a steady stream of headlights in the darkness.

The truth is, every one of the people in the airports, grocery stores, post offices, waiting rooms, and on the highway are human beings, just like you. And just like you, the context of their present moment is part of a long journey we call *life*. After they were born, they had the unique experiences we call childhood and adolescence. As adults, they have memories of this earlier time; and now they're struggling to stay safe, earn a living, raise a family, handle the challenges of relationships, deal with medical issues, and sort through the noise of culture to determine what is true.

Meanwhile, you're creating your life path one decision at a time. Your life is precious, and your journey is vastly important to you. We all share what we call our "common humanity." Every individual is a living, thinking and feeling being, with all the struggles and challenges of being alive and creating a life. Each of us has to react to unexpected problems, crises, or disasters. Somehow, we have to deal with it and make it through without hurting ourselves or anyone else. Everyone tries, but not everyone succeeds.

What's difficult to appreciate is that other people's lives are every bit as complex and precious as your own. No one has the same perceptions of reality or the same memories, thoughts, feelings, goals, relationships, character strengths, personalities, strengths, weaknesses, attitudes, values, knowledge, skills, or habits. No two people imagine the same things or dream the same dreams, during the day or while asleep.

In truth, we're more different than we are similar—amazingly so. And it's hard—no, virtually impossible—to truly understand what another person's life is like: what's happening to them today, what they're thinking and feeling right now, what their life journey has been, and what they hope will happen in the time they have left.

This creates a "separateness" that can only be mitigated by *communication*. Most of the time we don't make the effort to be truly aware of the people around us, their stories, and their challenges. This doesn't necessarily mean we're callous, but the danger is that we won't empathize with their situation and will fail to take their needs into account when we make decisions that impact them.

Organizations are made of people—each one a unique human being—and it helps to acknowledge what this means, rather than passing them in the hall or gazing back at them in meetings, while oversimplifying your perceptions, seeing them as a mere backdrop for your personal experience.

When you more fully appreciate the richness and the reality of an individual, it's much easier to treat them with compassion and respect. It's much easier to invest in the long-term commitment to improving the way you communicate with them, so they're encouraged and inspired to work with you, to do their best alongside you every day.

Teams exist for a reason. No matter how smart and skilled you are, you'll be given challenges you can't accomplish by yourself. To get the job done, you'll need capable people who are willing to work with you and give a maximum effort to accomplish an important mission.

And this can happen. It's possible to hire people who are capable of doing what needs to be done. But how will they respond to each other and to people in charge? Will they give their best effort day after day?

The answer will be *yes, they will, if they*:

- Know what's expected

- Know how to do it

- Have what they need to do it

- Want to do it

These are some big ifs. Sometimes supervisors don't have a clear notion of what will be perceived as success; or if they do, they may not communicate it well to the team. Or if team members really are talented, they may have something to say about what can be achieved, when and how. If they aren't given the opportunity to give their input, they may not fully buy into expectations. And when situations change, expectations may need to change.

Sometimes what needs to be done isn't well aligned with team members' experiences or skill sets. Often in such cases, managers take a "just do it" approach, expecting them to pick up the know-how while doing the work.

And not all managers fully appreciate how to empower employees. The people who do the work will need guidance, information, authority, resources, and other forms of support. A failure to provide any of these could be like trying to squeeze blood from a stone.

Still, even if a team is loaded with talent, knows what needs to be done, has the know-how and confidence to do it, and is empowered by support—even with all that—there could be reasons to withhold their best efforts.

One big question is trust. Giving 100% to accomplish a team goal is a two-way street. Will the people who work with you have your back? Will they shield you from criticism and pressure from above when there are unexpected problems? Will they take responsibility or will they blame others? Will they tell the truth, even if the truth puts them in a bad light? When projects succeed, will they recognize and reward other people's contributions? If you don't trust that your manager and team members will look out for your needs, why would you risk the extra effort to accomplish a difficult mission?

The bottom line is that if you fail to learn about your coworkers or communicate in ways that show your concern for them, you're unlikely to establish the kind of trusting relationships that inspire high levels of performance. Given how easy it is to withhold one's best efforts, we encourage you to commit to improving the skills that enable you to meaningfully connect with your coworkers.

This chapter in a nutshell:

- **People have talent and inner strength, and they have the potential to contribute at a very high level.**

- **But they have to know what's expected, how to perform the tasks, and be supported by empowerment. Most of all they have to want to give that much of themselves at work.**

- **Whether they decide to commit to this level of performance depends on how people interact with each other to create mutually supportive work relationships.**

Learn more about team motivation:

- John C. Maxwell, *Developing the Leader within You* (HarperCollins, 2019)

- Robin Sharma, *The Leader Who Had No Title* (Free Press, 2010)

- Thomas Gordon, *Leader Effectiveness Training* (TarcherPerigee, 2001)

"Make sure that team members know they are working with you, not for you."

John Wooden

"Those who enjoy responsibility usually get it, those who merely like exercising authority usually lose it."

Malcolm Forbes

2

....

Authority: How Power Can Let You Down

If you're a manager, you hold most of the high cards: knowledge of the business, connections, experience, resources, and authority. Did we forget something? Even though you may appreciate the talents of your team members, you have the clout to enforce policies, regulations, directions and orders. You're the law.

And the people around you know this.

Yes, there's more to relationships than the authority of your position, and this assessment of your power paints a severe picture. Not that you'll play the power cards in every situation. You may exercise compassion and understanding as a general rule. But when you're exhausted, have you ever been tempted to say, "Because I said so"?

It would only be natural if you did. Human beings are rational, far more so than any other species on Earth. But we're also an emotional species. When it seems as though everything in your day is one more challenge, one more assault on your equilibrium, the desire to vent or strike back is a natural emotional reaction. You may respond to someone's surprising and irrational behavior with shock, dismay, frustration, disappointment, or even anger. But people resent being treated this way.

Instinctive reactions take many forms. Here are some of the more hurtful ones.

Orders, commands, warnings, threats, and ultimatums

You may decide to make a change, but someone may resist it. To get your way, you can play the power card.

"I don't care if this is inconvenient. Just do it."

"For the hundredth time, make a record of those conversations."

"If you show up late one more time, you'll be looking for another job."

"Just so you understand: if you get reported for a violation, I'll pull your certification."

The message: *While you're working for me on this team, you'll do what I say.* Denny's wife once told him that her father used to say, "When I say 'jump,' you say 'how high' on the way up." Directives like this come from a manager's inherent power and authority. Exercising this authority doesn't promote a caring, trusting relationship. It doesn't nurture mutual respect and understanding. Adults want to be treated like adults—with consideration and respect. So naturally they resent the autocratic approach, in which they're treated as if they're inferior. When you lay down the law and make threats, the unspoken message is that you want to control others. The problem is, adults don't want to be controlled. They want to be encouraged and inspired, and ordering them around is a good way to erode the relationship.

Criticism, blame, shame, ridicule, insults, and sarcasm

People don't like verbal attacks; such comments imply that they lack intelligence and can't figure things out for themselves. Two bad things can happen. They could resent their leaders and brush off the abuse. Or worse, they might give credit to the attacks and suffer damage to their self-esteem.

"That attitude will get you nowhere."

"That was a dumb thing to do."

"It's your own fault."

"It's no wonder you're in such a mess."

"Don't be such a whiner."

"Oh that was cute. Nice move."

"You should be ashamed of yourself."

"The problem is, you're lazy."

Statements that imply someone is inadequate, incompetent, inept, incapable, or unworthy attack their motivation and self-esteem, which can have a negative impact on their performance.

Lecturing, preaching, debating, arguing, and giving advice

Many managers have been around long enough to believe they know what's best, and they may feel they're being helpful when they tell others what they should do. It might be hard to watch a team member struggle with a difficult situation. You have wisdom and experience, and you know that giving an answer or a solution can relieve anxiety and maybe teach something.

"Here's what you need to do...."

"If you want to do that, you'll have to prove to me you can handle it."

"That's not the way you act on this team."

"I think you're taking on too much."

"Let me tell you what's going on here."

"There's a lot better way to handle this."

Helping, solving, fixing, and giving advice—often with a good heart. Most of the time managers do, in fact, know best. But lecturing can send a demeaning message: *I'm smarter than you are, you're naïve, you're wrong, you don't know what you're doing, you'll fail without my help.*

When you take over someone's problem, it robs them of the opportunity to practice thinking and coping skills, and it promotes dependence when they should be learning to work independently. People become problem solvers by solving problems, and they gain self-confidence by achieving things through their own efforts.

Toxic questions

Sometimes name-calling and put-downs are implied in the questions leaders ask. It's a rare manager who has never said, "What's wrong with you?" or "Can't you follow simple instructions?"

These are what we call *toxic questions.*

"What's wrong with you?" implies a hurtful message: *You're flawed as a person. You're too dumb to do what's right, even after you've been told. There's something wrong with you.*

Or in a tired, overwhelmed moment a manager might say in a raised voice: "Why did you do that?" The question has no answer. But it carries a hidden message: *What you did is so stupid that I can't imagine why you, or anyone for that matter, would do that. You're incompetent.*

A regular diet of hidden messages like these may be indistinguishable from psychological abuse. Here are a few other common toxic messages:

"What do you think you're doing?"

"What on Earth were you thinking?"

"How many times do I have to tell you...?"

"What am I going to do with you?"

"Why don't you do what you're told?"

"What's your problem?"

People who ask questions like these don't expect answers. Instead, they're sending hurtful messages. Toxic questions strike at the heart of a person's self-esteem. So why say them? Maybe you felt tired and frustrated at the time and didn't recognize the hidden meaning. Or maybe you heard questions like these from your own managers when they were tired and frustrated.

Reacting emotionally can be destructive. When you lash out, people become less trusting. Coworkers might feel anger or even a loss of respect. This natural, automatic reaction to disappointment elevates the emotional quality of the situation and can leave others feeling inadequate. The consequences over time can be a gradual erosion of work relationships, not the team bonding you hope for. This isn't the kind of manager or coworker you want to be.

Improving workplace communication skills is a game-changer. The first step is to appreciate that your natural emotional reactivity can have bad consequences, and the authority of your position can lure you into believing you're justified in responding this way. The second step is to catch yourself when you feel your emotions boiling up. Then remember to do the hard thing, the more effective thing: *resist the impulse to express these emotions; then take a moment to calm yourself and consider ways to communicate effectively.*

The top 10 workplace communication skills

While there are dozens of so-called "people skills," Part Two of this book focuses on the 10 interpersonal skills that we feel give managers and coworkers the greatest positive impact to foster productive workplace relationships:

Listening to understand. Resist the impulse to talk, and start paying attention. Express empathy and check what you think your coworker is trying to say. The goal is to get the message, even if the person has trouble communicating it, and even if it's something you don't want to hear.

Coaching people to think for themselves. Instead of lecturing, instructing or giving advice, ask open-ended questions that get someone to form the habit of doing their own thinking. Encouraging someone to think is the No. 1 way you can cultivate their ability to exercise good judgment, problem-solving, and decision-making.

Guiding learning from experience. Successes, as well as mistakes and failures, happen all the time. Ideally, people learn from these experiences, but this doesn't always happen. You can help others reflect on what has happened to learn lessons that they can apply to similar situations in the future.

Getting buy-in for expectations. The traditional approach is to expect people to follow the directions of management. But you get a lot more enthusiasm for the work when you involve others in setting goals, objectives, and milestones.

Offering encouragement. Unexpected setbacks can sap morale. The stronger individuals may pick themselves up and drive on, but not everyone is so resilient. Encouragement is the cure, if done effectively.

Expressing appreciation. People want their hard work to be noticed and appreciated. Always a good idea: as often as possible, when someone does something well, mention the specific behaviors that pleased you. Do this more often than reacting to the negatives. Any sign of positive feedback is welcome, and there's a simple approach to having maximum impact.

Giving feedback constructively. First, acknowledge the positives in their behavior; then describe specifically the behavior that troubled you—and why. Next, describe the behavior you'd rather see. Give encouragement and affirm your confidence that the individual can meet your expectations.

Accepting feedback graciously. Criticism rarely feels good, and even constructive feedback that's intended to encourage can cause a negative reaction. The truth is, feedback is worth its weight in gold, and you don't want to discourage it by reacting badly. There are techniques for accepting feedback graciously.

Engaging in dialogue. Ask for people's opinions, and listen to understand without debating or criticizing. Even though you may not accept their reasoning, you can learn what they're thinking and even share your own point of view without trying to convince them that you're right. And you might pick up some helpful insights.

Resolving conflict creatively. The approach is to hear what the other person wants, then find out why—the needs that are driving their wants. Check to be sure you understand correctly. Then describe your own needs. Finally, get creative: together explore alternatives that will meet both your needs at the same time.

Your goal is to help the people around you be more successful while nurturing the kind of mutually supportive relationships that encourage them to open up about important issues, then deal with and resolve these issues. When people feel understood, respected, and supported, it has an amazing impact on teamwork and results.

The difference-maker is effective communication. The chapters in Part Two explain what you can do to master these skills. As you work on improving the way you communicate, there are a few things you need to keep in mind about building skills.

This chapter in a nutshell:

- **When someone disappoints you, it's natural to feel annoyed, irritated, or worse.**

- **The instinctive response is to express these negative emotions.**

- **Because of their position and authority, managers often feel that this kind of reaction is typical and expected.**

- **Communicating negatively attacks coworkers' self-esteem and motivation.**

- **To build people up and strengthen team relationships, the answer is to use a number of positive, empowering communication skills.**

Learn more about building work relationships:

- Christopher Kukk, *The Compassionate Achiever* (HarperCollins, 2017)

- Michael J. Gelb, *The Art of Connection* (New World Library, 2017)

- Thomas Gordon, *Leader Effectiveness Training* (TarcherPerigee, 2001)

"If you want to get good at anything where real-life performance matters, you have to actually practice that skill in context. Study, by itself, is never enough."

Josh Kaufman

3

....

The Secret to Improving Communication Skills

In Part Two you'll be encouraged to use the 10 most powerful communication skills with your team while dealing with workplace challenges. We'll introduce you to these skills and launch you on the journey of mastering them. How you handle these interactions could help people work through problems, improve skills, and build the kind of core strengths they'll need to do the hard things.

Along the way, you'll discover that these are the same skills that work with your family and friends.

No one likes to be discounted or talked down to. They don't like being given orders. They don't appreciate it when you push your agenda without hearing what they have to say. They resist people who disregard their needs. When you use these 10 adult-to-adult communication skills with your coworkers on a regular basis, some wonderful things can happen:

- When you demonstrate convincingly that you care about the people around you, they'll care about you. If you're listening to them, they'll want to listen to you. It's a matter of mutual respect. As you connect with your team members, team cohesion will grow stronger. As a consequence, you'll have more influence.

- You'll have a greater chance of avoiding issues, because your coworkers will help you see them coming, which will make it easier to implement solutions.

- When you use communication skills in your daily inter-actions, you'll be modeling the best ways of communi-cating. People learn a lot by observing what works, and you'll be setting an example for the best way to relate with each other—how to be an effective manager and team member. You'll be investing in their future success and job satisfaction.

- You'll be encouraging your team members to think for themselves to resolve issues independently.

As you'll see, the skills aren't complicated. But there's a "catch." *Mastering them requires a lot of practical application.* Learning about them—reading the chapters—is a great begin-ning. You'll become familiar with how they work and appreciate what they can do for you. But only if you use them on the job on a regular basis will you eventually make them your automatic, habitual way of relating to others.

How to rewire your brain for a new skill

When you improve a skill, in effect you're replacing a bad habit with a good one. It's the same process as when an athlete adopts a different, more effective technique; when someone gives up smoking; or when someone changes the way they eat. After you learn what you need to do, getting to the point where you can do it well and do it consistently is a journey. If you want to im-prove the way you communicate with your team members, you'll need to *make it a habit*—one that supersedes the old one.

There's a general misconception about learning a skill. Most people think that if you read the best book about it or go to an outstanding training course, value what you've learned, and even practice simulated exercises, you'll be able to change the way you do things on the job. Almost everyone thinks this is how it works, and we wish it were true. But it's not. Changing a lifelong behavior pattern takes more than having good intentions and knowing what to do. Reading a book, watching a video, or working with a coach can show you a better way of interacting with team members and can be a great beginning. The harder part of your challenge is to *consistently apply* what you've learned—to actually use the skill over and over in daily interactions.

> *Knowing how to do something and actually doing it aren't the same thing.*

The skill-building process for acquiring these skills is exactly like that of an athlete who's trying to master a better way of shooting a free-throw, hitting a golf ball out of a sand trap, or hitting a tennis ball backhand with topspin. After you've been shown what to do, you need practice, practice, and more practice. Each time you apply a new skill in the workplace, each "rep" stimulates the brain cells involved in the skill to continue growing towards each other until they're connected into a circuit. Further practice physically reinforces the circuit; myelin—which acts like insulation for an electric wire—surrounds the brain cells in the circuit. This allows electrochemical impulses to travel through the circuit at very high speeds. This process is why it takes so much practice to turn a skill into a habit—a comfortable, automatic behavior pattern.

And it needs to be a habit, because most of your daily interactions can't be driven by conscious decisions to communicate a certain way. In the busy flow of work, you'll need to react with the skill automatically. With enough application in the real world, the skill will eventually start to feel natural. When it does, you'll know your brain has been rewired, and you'll have replaced your old habitual way of responding with a new, improved one.

People replace bad habits with better ones all the time.

So, how do you change habits, when your brain is already physically wired to produce the problem behavior? It took years of repetitions to create the brain circuits for the work habits you have now. So naturally it will take a lot of "reps" to rewire the circuits for new skills. At first, you'll fight your old habit. In your everyday interactions, you'll try to remember what you learned and then concentrate on doing it that way. You'll pick yourself up from your mistakes and failures and keep trying. Like an athlete trying to improve skills, you'll do the work.

We're telling you this because when you read the next 10 chapters, you'll realize how powerful your interactions with coworkers can be. You'll "get it," and you'll be excited about what you're learning. It's important to follow through and persist, because rewiring your brain for improved communication skills can take months. Mastering all 10 of them—one at a time—could take years. It will depend on how many "reps" you're getting—how often you actually use the skills.

It's helpful to think that an old, ingrained habit is like a familiar, well-traveled road—how you usually get from Point A to Point B. You've used this route for so many years that the turns and stops are practically automatic. At some point, you realize that even though you feel like you could drive it in your sleep, the twists and turns are slowing you down and causing wear and tear. Like this old road, your habitual way of reacting causes problems for you and others.

And then one day you realize your journey will be far more enjoyable and effective if you have a better route. This will be like constructing a new highway. The better way to get to where you want to go will benefit you in lots of ways, but at first it will be under construction. In the early stages the going will sometimes be slow and confusing. But after the expressway is finished, your journey from Point A to Point B will be faster and safer. The old route will still be there, but you'll stop using it and eventually it will fall into disrepair.

It takes work to break a bad habit, and people do it all the time. Motivation helps. The process is easier if you understand how behavior change usually happens. This description of four stages of competence is adapted from Prochaska & DiClemente's "Transtheoretical Model":

1. **Unconscious incompetence.** Your habitual way of doing something doesn't work very well, but you aren't aware that it's causing problems or that there's a better way.

2. **Conscious incompetence.** If you're lucky, you'll find out that what you're doing is causing issues. Maybe the behavior causes distress or problems in your relationships. Maybe someone has given you feedback. You have not committed to change yet, but you're not blissfully unaware anymore.

3. **Conscious competence.** In this stage you learn what you should be doing instead, and you make an effort to change. At first, you have to concentrate in order to do something different. You haven't rewired your brain, so the new way isn't a habit yet. This is challenging because the old way is still an ingrained habit, still affecting your behavior.

   Knowledge and skills are stored as physical circuits in the brain. There's no delete switch; old habits are physically wired in your brain, so the circuits won't just disconnect themselves and go away. The trick is to repeat the new behavior so many times that your brain rewires itself for a new, more rewarding habit.

This new construction takes work. At first, you know what to do and you want to do it, but sometimes you forget. A situation happens and you react automatically with your old, familiar habit. When you realize your mistake later, you feel frustrated and discouraged. Or as you try focusing on one aspect of the skill, you overlook others. At this point you might blame the skill. You might rationalize that it just doesn't feel right. It's too hard. It's not going to work for you. You'll be tempted to give up.

4. **Unconscious competence.** Instead of giving up, you push past your lapses and consciously keep trying. Each effort stimulates the brain cells to connect, and after a while your success rate improves. You still have occasional shortfalls; but if you don't give up, if you keep trying, eventually your brain does rewire itself for the new habit. This means that doing the right thing begins to kick in automatically without a conscious effort on your part. The new behavior becomes the way you perform the skill—easily and comfortably.

This is how all skills are built and habits are formed—both good ones and bad ones. In the past, you probably formed most of your habits without realizing that you were doing so. To change them, you'll need to be self-aware. The concept may be simple, but you'll need to do the work. Even though your initial failures may be disheartening, accept that they're an inevitable part of the skill development process. And *don't give up.* You'll have some successes initially, and you'll have even more if you learn from your experiences and continue to use the skills.

The initial rough going happens to everybody. The secret is to learn from your mistakes. The most effective way to learn from experience is the Focus-Action-Reflection (FAR) approach:

1. **Focus.** Work on improving one skill at a time. You have a lot going on in your life, and working on one of the skills takes a fair amount of concentration and effort. Trying to improve more than one skill simultaneously will cause you to dilute your efforts.

2. **Action.** Once you understand what's involved in a skill, getting good at it means actually doing it, over and over. Practice, practice, and more practice.

3. **Reflection.** In spite of your best intentions, at first you'll miss opportunities to apply what you learned; and even if you do remember, you may not do it very well. If you reflect on your experiences, you can turn these shortfalls into learning.

The 5 magic reflection questions

Yes, experience is a great teacher, but people don't always learn from their mistakes. Sometimes they go from one unfortunate experience to another without learning a thing. For maximum learning, after a successful interaction, or one that didn't go well, take the time to answer these questions, preferably in this order:

1. **What happened?** The details of an event need to be recalled in order to make sense of them. What was the sequence of events? What did you do? How did others react? How do you feel about it?

2. **Why did you handle it this way?** Things happen for a reason. To imagine a better way to handle a situation like this, try to understand why things occurred the way they did. What were you thinking? What helped or hindered? What led to the outcome?

3. **What were the consequences?** Appreciating the impact of what happened creates the motivation to handle

situations like this more effectively. Benefits? Costs? Problems? Resolutions?

4. **How would you handle a similar situation in the future?** What did you learn from this experience? What basic principles? How are you going to apply the lesson?

5. **What are your next steps?** What will you do in the next 48 hours to set you up for implementing this learning?

Tips for optimum skill-building:

- **Record the lesson.** When reflecting on your mistakes, instead of just thinking about the answers to these questions, write them down. People think more thoroughly when they write, and having a record of your thoughts will allow you to review them later.

- **Persist.** In the beginning, it may seem as if you're having more failures than successes. Don't let this discourage you. Occasional lapses are par for the course. They happen to everybody, even elite athletes. Just keep trying and your success rate will gradually improve. The secret is simply to *refuse to give up*. Remember that if you give up, your chance to improve the way you connect with others in the workplace and reap the many benefits is lost.

- **Acknowledge improvement.** When you do remember to try the new way and experience some success, give yourself credit. Be conscious of your success rate, so you appreciate that progress is happening.

- **Get coaching.** It's hard to make it through the rewiring process without someone to encourage you to keep trying. It makes a big difference to have someone who cares about your success to listen to your frustrations, give feedback, encourage you, and hold you accountable. Over the long haul, this kind of support will help you work past discouragement and ingrain the new behaviors. The best coach could be your manager, because this person observes your work on a regular basis. Ideally your manager has read this book and is embarking on a similar journey to improve communication. Or a colleague can learn with you, help you set goals, encourage you, and hold you accountable. And of course, if it's in your budget, you can work with a professional coach.

With enough successful encounters, the new way will start to feel natural. Once you notice that you don't have to concentrate to do it, and using the skill feels comfortable and automatic, you'll have rewired your brain. You'll "own" the new skill.

This realistic perspective on adopting new behavior patterns will help you master the game-changing ways to communicate in the workplace. These skills are described in the next 10 chapters, beginning with the foundation skill: *listening to understand.*

This chapter in a nutshell:

- **Knowing what to do and actually doing it aren't the same thing.**

- **Changing the way you communicate means re-wiring your brain.**

- **Repetition is the key to ingraining a new habit.**

- **The best approach is to work on one skill at a time.**

- **In spite of your best intentions, at first your old habits will kick in.**

- **Reflect on your shortfalls, learn from them, and rededicate yourself.**

- **If you consistently make the effort to apply what you've learned and if you persist through frustration, the new skill will become your habitual way of communicating.**

- **It helps to have a coach to hold you accountable and offer encouragement.**

Learn more about skill-building:

- Charles Duhigg, *The Power of Habit* (Random House, 2012)

- Robin Sharma, *The 5 AM Club* (HarperCollins, 2018)

- Benjamin Hardy, *Willpower Doesn't Work* (Hatchette Books, 2018)

- Robert Maurer, *One Small Step Can Change Your Life* (Workman Publishing, 2014)

....

PART TWO

The Top 10 Relationship-building Skills

We've been helping adults learn interpersonal skills for decades, and we're aware that there are dozens of such skills. The 10 skills that are the focus of this book have the greatest potential to help build relationships while encouraging high levels of performance.

These are the skills that foster engagement, build team cohesion, and grow a culture of coaching and compassion:

- Listen to understand

- Coach people to think for themselves

- Guide learning from experience

- Get buy-in for expectations

- Offer encouragement

- Express appreciation

- Give feedback constructively

- Accept feedback graciously

- Engage in dialogue

- Resolve conflict creatively

"Most people do not listen with the intent to understand; they listen with the intent to speak."

Stephen Covey

"You can see a lot, just by listening."

Yogi Berra

4

....

Listen to Understand

The heart of the skill described in this chapter was first called "active listening" by Thomas Gordon, who made it the centerpiece of his 1970 book, *P.E.T – Parent Effectiveness Training*. This way of listening, adapted from techniques used by therapists and counselors, has also been referred to as "reflective listening" and "empathic listening." We prefer Stephen Covey's term: "listening to understand."

Listening to understand is the most important aspect of effective team communication.

Whatever your reason for communicating, you won't be doing all the talking. The people around you often have something to say that can influence your team's success, and you'll need to hear it. Knowing they've been heard and understood has a powerful effect on people. When others sense that their ideas, issues, and observations are being considered, they feel valued and appreciated.

Also, the ability to grasp what someone is trying to say is a critical component of the other nine communication skills featured in this book. This is why we encourage you to work on listening first.

People won't make it easy for you to listen well. Sometimes they aren't confident about how to bring up issues. As they deal with problems, mistakes, and conflicts, they may keep their thoughts and feelings to themselves. And if they do open up, it's almost never in the form of a logical, well-organized speech. The points they're trying to make, which they may not fully grasp themselves, could be heavily laced with emotion and mixed with anecdotes, opinions, complaints, demands, and feelings—in no particular order. They might start with whatever is on their mind and go from there. Along the way, they might digress. As a result, the meaning could be hard to sort out.

If you aren't a skilled listener—and most people aren't—you may end up doing more talking than listening, reacting with your own feelings, seeing the situation from your own point of view, and misinterpreting the other person's message.

The consequences of a failure to communicate can be huge. For one thing, you'll miss an opportunity to learn about issues festering in the workplace. If your coworkers sense that you don't understand what they're trying to tell you, they may conclude you don't care and decide it's too hard to get through to you. Your team members might feel disrespected and misunderstood and wonder if coming to you with issues is worth the effort. Consequently, the relationships that are so important to teamwork could begin to unravel. Poor listening is one of the main reasons people distance themselves from their managers and coworkers.

Consider this situation, in which a team leader changes a technician's priorities:

Technician: "You wanted to see me?"

Team Leader: "Are you on the Wayne project this morning?"

Technician: "I am. Leaving now."

48

Team Leader: "No, don't leave yet. I want you to do something else."

Technician: "What?"

Team Leader: "We have a new customer, We Got Flowers. I want you to go out there with Fremont, take measurements, and start removing their storeroom flooring."

Technician: "But that could take all day."

Team Leader: "Right. Just do it, okay?"

Technician: "But we have an appointment with Wayne, and..."

Team Leader: "I know. Just handle it."

Technician: "But..."

Team Leader: "Look, I don't have time for this. Here's the order. Take Fremont and get started."

Technician: "This is the second time, and..."

Team Leader: "We need this new customer. Just do it!"

Technician: "Okay."

What the technician tried to explain was that she had already rescheduled the Wayne project once, and the customer had agreed to meet that morning to finish the job and would be irate if rescheduled again. Wayne Auto Repair has six other locations in the area, and a disgruntled customer could mean negative word of mouth. The technician wanted to talk about a way to make both customers happy, but the team leader didn't give her a chance. He cut her off and gave her the new marching orders.

The team leader was working from a traditional mindset of exercising authority. In his mind, he was doing the right thing for the company. As a result, in trying to satisfy a new customer, he was about to disappoint an existing one. If he had given the technician a chance to speak, things might have turned out differently.

Like many leaders, he had never had training in how to listen. And yet, even people who've had this training and have tried to practice the skills on the job often discover how hard it is to simply recognize the opportunities for using them. That's when old habits kick in. Instead of listening for the meaning and checking for understanding, they exercise their authority, cut people off, and give orders.

Old habits can kick in while talking to family members, too. When Meredith's daughter Alison was in high school, she used to babysit after school to earn spending money. One afternoon she had a difficult situation with one of the children, and she was upset when she got home. As Meredith listened to Alison describe what happened, she jumped into problem-solving mode, asking a lot of questions and then offering ideas about how Alison might have handled the situation differently. As Alison continued to talk about her experience, Meredith continued to offer advice.

Finally, Alison said very emphatically, *"Mom, I don't need your suggestions. I had a horrible day. All I really wanted you to do is listen and be sympathetic. I've already taken care of this."* These words stopped Meredith in her tracks. She realized Alison was looking for understanding and compassion, not criticism or advice.

All these years later, Meredith still remembers how easy it was to disregard her own guidance about best listening practices. That's why we emphasize that mastering listening and the other skills is a *lifetime* pursuit.

Listening moments and the listening mindset

The first step to listening well is being aware of when to listen—what we call "listening moments"—when somebody is trying to tell you something. Also, these might be occasions when what someone does takes you by surprise: unexpected problems, conflicts, mistakes in judgment, or a point of view contrary to your own. You'll feel your own response: disappointment, frustration, or anger. These feelings are your signal that *this is a listening moment*, not an occasion to react. Once you realize you need to be listening, the next step is to check that you're in the proper frame of mind for listening—what we call the "listening mindset."

Recognize the "listening moment"

...when someone is trying to tell you something you need to hear.

Engage your "listening mindset"

I care about this person's problems, thoughts, and feelings. Something is going on with them right now, and I want to know what it is. So rather than react negatively or assume I understand, I check what I'm hearing.

Thinking these thoughts at the right time will be like having your relationship radar set at the right listening frequency, preparing you for effective listening. Actually, listening to understand involves four skills:

1. **Give your undivided attention.**

2. **Sense what the other person is feeling and express empathy.**

3. **Listen for the meaning and check what you think you understand.**

4. Encourage the person to continue talking until you're sure you understand what they're trying to say.

Listening skill 1: Give your undivided attention.

In his book, *What Got You Here Won't Get You There*, executive coach Marshall Goldsmith says that former president Bill Clinton was an "absolute master" at giving his attention to anyone who spoke to him. "He acted as if you were the only person in the room. Every fiber of his being, from his eyes to his body language, communicated that he was locked into what you were saying. He conveyed how important you were, not how important he was."

Whether someone is venting or you sense something is bothering them, this is an opportunity to demonstrate that you genuinely care about what they're trying to say, that they can get through to you. Once you realize that this is a listening moment and your mind is set for listening, make finding out what's going on your top priority. Stop what you're doing and do what Bill Clinton is said to have done: *consciously focus 100% on the other person.*

Multi-tasking or fiddling with objects will distract your attention. Put down your phone, book or pen, and turn to face the other person. Try to keep your mind clear, because even your thoughts, feelings, opinions, memories, and imagination can distract you from hearing what they're saying. If necessary, invite them to talk with you in another room or outside where you can face each other in relative quiet and privacy. Communicate through your posture and facial expressions that *this is the most important person in your world right now.* From time to time, give them an accepting smile, a nod, or an occasional "yes" or "I see" to affirm that you're focused and listening.

Listening skill 2: Sense what the other person is feeling and express empathy.

Most of the time, what you sense will be a combination of thoughts and emotions. Sometimes a person will lead with what they're feeling. Many of the opportunities to connect with someone will be triggered by feelings such as delight or frustration. Other times they'll be able to speak in a rational way. Even then, you may pick up on how they feel about it. Showing you understand their needs and feelings will make it easier for them to open up.

Mindfulness is a crucial first step to expressing empathy. Mindfulness means focusing on the present moment to be fully aware of what's in front of you. No one is in this state of mind all the time. During a busy day, most people only intermittently experience moments of intense mindfulness. When you're solving problems, planning, and executing, you may be aware of the people around you, but in a kind of distant way. This is normal.

Before expressing empathy, you need to experience it. And to experience empathy, you need to be mindful of the other person, focusing on what they are experiencing and feeling. This means shifting from your own thoughts and feelings to sensing the other person in the here-and-now. Your concern is most real and intense when you're able to experience someone else without the filter of whatever may be going on in your mind, without judging, reacting, thinking about something that happened, or paying attention to your own thoughts and feelings. Only when you're mindfully aware of the other person is an empathic connection possible.

Mark Goulston, in his book, *Just Listen*, says this:

"Making someone 'feel felt' simply means putting yourself in the other person's shoes. When you succeed, you can change the dynamics of a relationship in a heartbeat. At that instant, instead of trying to get the better of each other,

you 'get' each other and the breakthrough can lead to cooperation, collaboration, and effective communication."

In our experience, expressing empathy follows three steps:

1. **Be "in the moment" with the person.** Empty your mind of every thought and feeling about what may have happened. Approach the person and the situation with fresh awareness. Consciously focus on the individual in the present moment. Observe facial expressions, posture, gestures, and tone of voice.

2. **Imagine what they're feeling.** Put yourself in their situation—not to agree or disagree, and not to judge, but simply to be aware of and understand what they're experiencing.

3. **Three ways to say what you imagine they're feeling.**

   - *Ask:* "Are you disappointed that we have to redo this?"

   - *Assume:* "You must be disappointed that we have to redo this."

   - *Express the feeling:* "It's disappointing to have to go back to square one and start over."

Listening skill 3: Listen for the meaning and check what you think you understand.

The biggest mistake people make when listening is assuming they understand what the other person is trying to say. The truth is, even skilled communicators sometimes miss the point. So with your attention focused on what the other person is saying, *listen for the meaning.* Interpret both the verbal and nonverbal messages, and ask yourself: *Why are they telling me this?* And when you think you understand some of what the person is expressing, check to be sure. The skill: *In your own words, say what you think you've understood so far.*

"Are you saying that...?"

"Do you mean that...?"

"It sounds like...."

"So what you're getting at is...."

"Let me see if I heard you right. You...."

The skill is *not* to repeat verbatim what someone has said. Instead, express what you think they're getting at—the *meaning* of what they've said. Don't worry that you'll get it wrong. The important thing is to *check your understanding*. If your interpretation even slightly misses the point, the person will let you know. They may even correct you. As they try to explain, continue listening for the meaning and once again check what you think you understand.

Listening skill 4: Encourage the person to continue talking until you're sure you understand what they're trying to say.

Most of the time you won't hear the whole story all at once. Even if someone verifies that you've correctly understood what you've heard so far, they may not have gotten to the main point. They probably have more to say. You may have to check your understanding several times before getting to the core of the issue.

So ask another open-ended question to encourage the person to continue talking—not so you can offer your opinion or advice, but to be sure you heard the whole story. Remember, an open-ended question is the kind of question that gets the speaker to say what's on their mind. It doesn't ask for specific information, which can be given in a one- or two-word answer, such as "No," or "Twice," or "Mr. Howard." Replies to factual questions tend to halt an interchange rather than keep it going. Some examples of how to encourage someone to say more:

"Go on."

"Please continue."

"And then what happened?"

"So, what do you think?"

"Why do you think he did that?"

"How do you feel about that?"

"How important is this to you?"

"What other issues do you see?"

"Why do you think this is your best option?"

"How will this affect your decision?"

"What's your plan?"

Sometimes you can tell when someone is having a bad day but isn't saying anything. Showing that you've noticed can get them to open up. This may create a listening moment.

You: "You seem upset. What's going on?"

Coworker: "Nothing."

You: "You don't seem like your usual self. Is something bothering you?" (CHECKING NONVERBAL MESSAGE)

Coworker: "No, not really."

You: "Okay, it sure seems like something's going on. You can tell me."

Coworker: "It's just some stupid thing. I saw Craig give erroneous information to a customer and when I confronted him about it, he said he didn't know what I was talking about."

You: "Why do you think he said that?" (OPEN-ENDED QUESTION)

Coworker: "Maybe he was embarrassed that I saw him do it."

You: "So you're bummed about it." (CHECKING MESSAGE)

Coworker: "Yeah, I guess so."

You: "What do you plan to do?"

Coworker: "Nothing. It's water under the bridge."

You: "You plan to continue teaming with Craig."

Coworker: "I guess so. But I'm not sure I trust him now."

You: "I see. You aren't sure he'll always give customers what they need." (CHECKING MESSAGE)

Coworker: "Right."

You: "How are you going to resolve this?" (OPEN-ENDED QUESTION)

Coworker: "I'm not sure. I guess I'll need to bring it up to him again. Maybe we can actually talk about it."

The magical thing about this way of listening is that when someone verifies your interpretation, *you know that they feel they've been heard and understood*, which inspires a feeling of connectedness that reinforces your relationship. And when you encourage someone to think through their problems (without offering your own solutions), you help them exercise critical thinking.

Listening this way often has a wonderful bonus: it can help the other person clarify their thinking. When they open up to you, at first they may be distressed, but they may not know exactly what's bothering them. They may be anxious or upset and not know why. When you achieve an understanding of what's bothering them, this could be a useful revelation for them, too.

If you're like most people, listening to understand will mean replacing old communication habits with new ones. This means time, effort and persistence, because your old habits are physically wired as circuits of your brain. Once again, if you sometimes forget to listen to understand, or if your efforts seem awkward, this is a normal aspect of the skill-building process. As we emphasized in Chapter 3 ("The Secret to Improving Communication Skills"), *the key is to keep trying*. If you stick with it, using the skill will begin to feel easier and more natural.

Let's revisit that interchange between the team leader and the technician...

Technician: "You wanted to see me?"

Team Leader: "Are you on the Wayne project this morning?"

Technician: "I am. Leaving now."

Team Leader: "No, don't leave yet. I want you to do something else."

Technician: "What?"

Team Leader: "We have a new customer, We Got Flowers. I want you to go out there with Fremont, take measurements, and start removing their storeroom flooring."

Technician: "But that could take all day."

Team Leader: "Right. Just do it, okay?"

Technician: "But we have an appointment with Wayne, and it could be really bad for us if we don't show up."

Team Leader: "Why do you say that?" (OPEN-ENDED QUESTION)

Technician: "Because we put him off before. This is our re-scheduled appointment. There are six other Wayne shops in the area, and it could be really bad for business if we get nasty word of mouth."

Team Leader: "I hear what you're saying. We don't want Wayne Auto to get irate. But we need this new customer. What can we do to make a good impression with both of them? Any ideas?" (OPEN-ENDED QUESTION)

Technician: "Maybe Fremont can go to Wayne and get started, while I take measurements at the flower shop. I can schedule a follow-up and then get over to Wayne Auto to help Fremont finish."

Team Leader: "You know, that sounds like a plan. Good thinking. Call me if you need help."

You may have to work to understand what someone is trying to say, but it's worth it. In this version, the team leader didn't cut the technician off or simply give orders. Instead, he listened and showed he understood. He asked for ideas and heard a solution that promised to resolve the conflict.

Tips for optimum listening:

- **Watch out for your emotional reactions.** Old habits die hard, and when someone annoys or upsets you, you may catch yourself reacting emotionally or falling back on authority. The feeling of rising emotions is usually a signal to listen instead.

- **Review your "listening mindset."** You may have trouble engaging the right mindset for listening if you're not clear what it is.

- **Be careful not to engage in conversation when you need to be listening.** Think of conversation and listening as two different things. Conversation involves sharing each other's stories, opinions, etc. It's a great way to nurture a connection with someone. There's a time to enjoy conversation and a time to focus on listening. Sometimes when you're just talking, you'll sense that your coworker wants to tell you something. If you understand the difference between conversation and listening, you can consciously shift into a listening mode.

- **Don't interrupt.** Listening is about the other person, not you. Interrupting to offer your own input will make it hard for them to complete their thought. Also, it implies that what you have to say is more important than what they have to say. Remember: your job is to understand, so the other person should be doing most of the talking.

- **Be flexible about how you use the four skills.** One good approach is to follow the skills in sequence. However, after you've become aware of a listening moment and have engaged your listening mindset, sometimes performing any one of the four skills in isolation can be effective. For example, expressing empathy is a powerful way of connecting and in certain situations can, by itself, achieve the understanding you seek. The same is true of listening for the meaning and checking the message. If the issue your coworker is struggling with isn't an emotional one, expressing empathy may not be needed. And if you're lucky, the message will be a straightforward one, and the other person can get to the point without further discussion. Even if you skip the empathy step, you can use it later in your listening if you sense that the emotional element is more of a factor than you initially thought. At other times, simply encouraging someone to continue speaking can be enough for them to clarify their thinking and even achieve a resolution.

- **Don't offer your experience, advice or solutions.** Once you understand the other person's issue, it can be a mistake to feel responsible for resolving it. You may have more experience and know-how. But as adults they're capable of figuring out how to deal with their issues, and doing so will help reinforce their problem-solving skills. You may sense that the solution they come up with might not work, and you'll be tempted to suggest a better approach. Giving advice and offering solutions can inhibit people from thinking creatively about options. Unless their solution has grave consequences, consider giving the person the opportunity to take responsibility for their work and learn from mistakes. You encourage people to think for themselves when you ask open-ended questions about the root of the problem, possible solutions, their ultimate decision, and their action steps.

- **Keep an open mind. Don't disagree, take offense or argue.** You may hear opinions or ideas that surprise you. Rather than reacting negatively, which would block communication, consider this an opportunity to combine listening with dialogue (more on this in Chapter 12, "Engage in Dialogue"). For example: If someone offers an idea that bothers you, instead of rejecting or criticizing it, respond with listening to make sure you understand what the person is suggesting. Then do three things: (1) state what you like about the idea (there are no perfectly good or perfectly bad ideas!); (2) explain your concerns; and (3) ask if the person is interested in exploring ways to improve the idea to address the concerns.

- **When listening to someone, be patient.** It may be as hard for them to explain what's on their mind as it is for you to grasp the explanation. It's a rare individual who gets straight to the point.

- **Look for listening moments when using other skills.** In the chapters ahead, you'll learn that listening is a key element of other communication skills, such as coaching someone to think, giving feedback, offering encouragement, engaging in dialogue, and resolving conflict. Each of these skills can stimulate someone to talk, so each could produce a special "listening moment."

- **Remember that becoming a more effective listener is a journey.** While this approach to listening to understand is very effective, it takes practice to get comfortable with it. The first few times you try using the skill, it won't feel natural. But keep at it. The more experience you gain, the more your confidence will build. The key is not to expect a 100% success rate at first. Give yourself credit for your successful efforts—good advice for learning any skill. The more you apply the skill, the easier it will get and the more often you'll experience success. No matter how many times you miss an opportunity to listen or forget to use one of the skills, recognize what happened and tell yourself to apply the skill next time. You can always revisit this chapter to remind yourself of what to do. With experience, you'll be the kind of listener your team needs you to be.

- **Keep the goal in mind.** Listening to understand is one of those skills, like chess or tennis, that you can continue to improve indefinitely. The better you get at it, the more your coworkers will open up to you, because they'll feel they've been heard, understood, and respected. Their self-esteem and the bond between you will grow stronger.

To get your "reps," stay alert for listening moments like these:

- The golden opportunity: someone comes to you wanting to talk

- When you try using one of the listening skills and the person responds

- You and your coworker disagree

- They make a case for something they want

- You give feedback and they get defensive

- You notice a change in mood, either positive or negative

- After asking an open-ended question, listen to understand the answer

This chapter in a nutshell:

- **Listening effectively is a vital component of many other communication skills.**

- **Listening well is how you find out what's happening with your coworkers. Also, it causes them to feel understood and appreciated, which promotes strong workplace relationships.**

- **Recognize when you need to listen—listening moments—and engage the right attitude—the listening mindset.**

- **Effective listening begins with giving your undivided attention.**

- **When you express empathy, you learn what your coworkers are feeling.**

- **When you check for understanding, you learn what your coworkers are trying to say.**

- **It may take a while to hear the whole message, so encourage the speaker to continue.**

Learn more about listening:

- Mark Goulston, *Just Listen* (Amacom, 2015)

- Thomas Gordon, *Leader Effectiveness Training* (TarcherPerigee, 2001), Chapters 4 and 5

- Marshall Goldsmith, *What Got You Here Won't Get You There* (Hyperion, 2007), Chapter 9

- Stephen R. Covey, *The 7 Habits of Highly Effective People,* Revised Ed. (Free Press, 2004), Habit 5

- Michael J. Gelb, *The Art of Connection* (New World Library, 2017), Chapter 6

*"Education is not the learning of facts,
but the training of the mind to think."*

Albert Einstein

5

....

Coach People to Think for Themselves

The best kind of teamwork depends on people who can deal with unexpected challenges and problems independently. You need people around you who do more than just react. You want them to see potential problems before they happen and, if necessary, deal with them logically and creatively. You need co-workers who can:

- Solve problems that come up every day

- Remain calm and effective in a crisis

- Manage resources

- Understand how team roles function to achieve team goals

- Create cooperative, mutually supportive relationships

- Learn new skills

Do you want others to always come to you with their problems, expecting you to give them a solution? This might satisfy your ego, but consider how effective a team would be if each person just confronted a problem, thought it through, decided what to do, and then took action. And when things don't turn out as planned, they learn from the effort and try something else.

But not everyone has this capacity. The ability to cope in a busy workplace requires a variety of creative and critical thinking skills. Not everyone acquires an impressive array of these skills as a part of growing up. You can help your team members improve these skills by encouraging them to think for themselves. The basic approach is simple:

Ask open-ended questions that get your team members to think.

An open-ended question is one that can't be answered with a simple "yes" or "no" or a word or two. This fairly simple communication technique is the opposite of always using your superior knowledge and experience to give answers and advice. Doing the thinking for them might resolve an immediate issue, but it won't encourage the growth of their own brain circuits for thinking.

The first step is to notice opportunities to coach them to think:

Recognize the "thinking moment"

...when you can encourage someone to do their own thinking, rather than give them the answer or solution.

Engage your "thinking mindset"

I ask open-ended questions that encourage my team members to practice thinking: understanding, reasoning, evaluating, problem-solving, decision-making, goal-setting, planning, and organizing.

Open-ended questions can take many forms, depending on the situation. Here are some classic opportunities for helping your team members wire their brain for patterns of good judgment and decision-making, along with examples of open-ended questions.

When you want your coworker to FORESEE CONSEQUENCES...

Knowing that a specific action causes a certain result requires imagining something that hasn't happened yet. If someone has observed cause and effect in the past, they can apply their memory of the incident to a similar situation in the present.

For example, say your team member wants to rent a van instead of buying one.

"What impact will this have on our budget?"

"What benefits do you foresee?"

"What downsides are there to renting?"

The idea is to get the person to think about what causes things to happen and to imagine what might happen as a result of their actions. This mental skill is vital to good judgment and decision-making. Typical questions:

"In this situation, what do you think will happen?"

"What do you hope to get out of this?"

"What's the payoff for finishing this?"

"How will this help you achieve your goal?"

"If you do this, what could happen next?"

"What other ways can you get what you want?"

"What could get in your way?"

"Why doesn't this feel right to you?"

"Based on what you know about her, what do you think she'll say?"

"What bad things might happen if you do what you're thinking about doing?"

"What would happen if you wait to say or do something?"

When you want your coworker to EVALUATE something...

One aspect of good judgment is the ability to appreciate the better option—the ability to assess the value of something. You can help your coworker become a more discerning thinker by asking questions such as:

"How are these three options different?"

"What does this do for you?"

"Why do you think [A] makes more sense than [B]?"

"What are the advantages of doing this?"

"What are the downsides?"

"What do you like most about that?"

"What are its best features?"

"What's wrong with it?"

"How well does it do what it's supposed to do?"

"Why do you think this is worth the price?"

"How safe is this?"

"How is this good for us?"

"How well does that person do this?"

"What do you think about how well this is made?"

Guide your coworker to THINK THROUGH PROBLEMS AND CHALLENGES...

Say your coworker is upset because they forgot they promised to help another team member work on a project, but then arranged to meet someone else at the same time. Or they want to buy an expensive item that's not in the budget. Or they put off doing an urgent task. Typical questions:

"What's the root problem?"

"What do you think went wrong?"

"How have you dealt with situations like this in the past?"

"What options do you have?"

"What's possible in this situation?"

"Which is more important to you, [...] or [...]?"

"Is there an even better way to [...]?"

"Why do you feel that this option is the best one?"

"If you do that, how will it meet your needs?"

"How will doing this benefit the other people involved?"

"What are the potential dangers?"

"What could this end up costing us?"

"Is there an option that will be acceptable to everyone?"

"What does your gut tell you?"

"To address this problem, what should you do first?"

"What can you do next to get back on track?"

"What can you postpone until later?"

The idea is to ask questions that lead your coworker to go through the typical steps of problem-solving: identifying the real problem, thinking of possible solutions, considering the pros and cons of each option, picking the best one, and making a plan. Even though you have lots of experience, keep in mind that it's your team member's problem as much as yours. Recognize the opportunity for them to exercise problem-solving skills, and resist the temptation to push your idea of the best solution.

You: "You seem down today."

Coworker: "CC Industries didn't pick us to do the work."

You: "I know. I'm sorry. I know you worked hard on it."

Coworker: "They picked Gazelle."

You: "How do you feel about that?"

Coworker: "Well, I was counting on doing that project. Now I don't know what to do."

You: "I know you had your heart set on it. What other prospects do you have in mind?"

Coworker: "I don't know. None."

You: "What can you do to find new prospects?"

Coworker: "I guess I could talk to some friends of mine."

You: "You never know what you might learn."

Coworker: "Or I could just call on some of our past customers."

You: "Does that sound promising?"

Coworker: "I think it's worth a try. We have good relationships."

You: "I agree. Do you have other options?"

Coworker: "CC Industries has some good competition in town."

You: "So you're going to pay them a visit?"

Coworker: "Yeah. And while I'm at it, I'll go talk to my friend Pat McLaren in the Chamber. She's kind of plugged in."

You: "Go for it."

When your coworker needs to SET GOALS AND MAKE PLANS...

Sometimes a goal or project requires team members to have specific roles. But will they think through how to succeed in their roles? To get there from here will involve a number of steps. If they have a plan and follow it, they're more likely to succeed. Once they begin thinking about goals, they can envision how to make it happen. Typical questions:

"What would you like to achieve on this project?"

"What will you need to do to get that?"

"What's most important to you?"

"What is your No. 1 goal right now?"

"How do you plan to begin if your project gets approved?"

"What do you want to do after this is over?"

"What are your options?"

"How much will this cost us?"

"What are the advantages and disadvantages of your plan?"

"How will doing this benefit us?"

"What will you need to do to achieve that?"

"What would be your best first step?"

"What's the hardest challenge you'll have to face?"

"If this happens, how will you deal with it?"

"What help or resources will you need?"

"If you go with this plan, how do you think it will work out?"

It can help if your coworker writes down a sequence of action steps. If they write each necessary action on a post-it note, they can easily rearrange them in time or cause-and-effect sequence. Listen to clarify what they say, rather than lecturing, explaining, or trying to solve their problem. In other words, ask questions to get them to do the planning.

You: "Are you looking forward to moving into our new space?"

Coworker: "Definitely."

You: "I'm going to need your help."

Coworker: "What do you mean?"

You: "You know, I have a lot on my plate right now. So, I'd like you to figure out what we're going to need to make the move happen—from start to finish. We need to be out of here a week from Friday. I need you to create a detailed plan so we meet that deadline. Can you do that?"

Coworker: "Sure."

A few days later, your coworker asks, "Do you think we should buy some new furniture?"

You: "What do you think?"

Coworker: "Maybe. But which items do you want me to buy?"

You: "Well there's four of us and you've seen the space. I'm sure you can figure out what we need."

To help people get more "reps," stay alert for thinking moments like these:

- You sense a potential problem situation, but you're concerned that your coworker doesn't appreciate the consequences

- Your coworker has a problem

- Your coworker is facing a difficult decision

- Your coworker has come up with a terrific creative idea but hasn't thought through what's required to make it happen

All the questions suggested in this chapter are variations of *What do you think?* When there's an opportunity to ponder, discover, think ahead, learn, plan, or deal with problems, you can ask open-ended questions that coach people to think for themselves. We've emphasized that you have to "do the work" to wire your brain for a new skill. This is true of thinking skills, too. Asking open-ended questions is a simple but powerful way to encourage this practice. And each time you ask for your coworker's thoughts, you'll send the message that you value their input, which will build their self-confidence and your relationship with them.

This chapter in a nutshell:

- **It's a real advantage to be surrounded by people who think well.**

- **There are lots of ways to encourage coworkers to improve their thinking.**

- **The key is asking open-ended questions—countless variations of *What do you think?***

Learn more about encouraging people to think for themselves:

- David Rock, *Quiet Leadership* (Harper Business, 2007)

- David Rock and Linda Page, *Coaching with the Brain in Mind* (Wiley, 2009)

- Michael Bungay Stanier, *The Coaching Habit* (Box of Crayons Press, 2016)

"There are no mistakes or failures, only lessons."

Denis Waitley

6

....

Guide Learning from Experience

The previous chapter introduced you to several ways to get others in the habit of thinking for themselves. The obvious benefit of doing this is to help coworkers work smarter.

One of the most valuable opportunities for helping people think for themselves is to get them in the habit of analyzing the good things and the bad things that happen on the job. It's often said that experience is the best teacher and that the value of mistakes is that you can learn from them.

There's a lot of wisdom in this. And to capture the lessons, a person has to think about what happened and why. People sometimes experience success; but they don't always think about what worked so they can repeat the success in the future.

And when they fall short, they don't always analyze why. Learning from mistakes doesn't happen automatically. In a busy workplace it's all too easy to go from situation to situation without giving much thought to what happened. But if they don't learn from their shortfalls, people are more likely to repeat their mistakes.

Consciously learning from experience not only helps people stay on track and do what works, it actually accelerates skill development. These are compelling reasons to make a habit of reflecting on why things happen the way they do. As a manager or concerned team member, you can encourage the people around you to do this.

The key is to get good at spotting a "learning moment"—when something significant has happened, whether it's a success or a failure. When you sense excitement, agitation, anger or frustration, this is your hint to take a few moments to ask the questions that will help others learn from their experience.

Recognize the "learning moment"

...when something significant has happened, and your coworker can learn from it.

Engage your "learning mindset"

I ask open-ended questions that encourage my team members to analyze what happened so they can improve the way they approach their work in the future.

Learning from experience is about on-the-job learning: quickly making a conscious effort to mine what has happened at work and discovering the lessons that lead to improvement. You do this by asking these open-ended questions:

1. **What happened?** The details of an event need to be recalled in order to make sense of them. What was the sequence of events? What did you do? How did others react? How do you feel about it?

2. **Why did you handle it this way?** Things happen for a reason. To imagine a better way to handle a situation like this, try to understand why things occurred the way they did. What were you thinking? What helped or hindered? What led to the outcome?

3. **What were the consequences?** Appreciating the impact of what happened creates the motivation to handle situations like this more effectively. Benefits? Costs? Problems? Resolutions?

4. **How would you handle a similar situation in the future?** What did you learn from this experience? What basic principles? How are you going to apply the lesson?

5. **What are your next steps?** What will you do in the next 48 hours to set you up for implementing this learning?

This exercise forces you to discover the lesson embedded in any significant experience. You can also help others learn from what has happened by asking open-ended questions that will cause them to reflect. The exchange needs to take the form of a discussion, not a lecture. You can be the one to ask the questions, while encouraging them to do most of the talking. Even if the insight is perfectly clear to you, when the learning comes from them it has far greater impact. A typical scenario:

Manager: "You seem upset about something."

Coworker: "No, I'm okay."

Manager: "You don't look happy. Tell me what happened."

Coworker: "It's no big deal. The contractor did his work, but the customer inspected it before I did, and now he's complaining."

Manager: "What did the contractor do?"

Coworker: "He subbed the work to another guy who apparently did a sloppy job."

Manager: "What do you think was the sub's problem?"

Coworker: "I don't know. Maybe he wasn't experienced. Maybe the contractor should have used someone else. Maybe he should have supervised him better."

Manager: "So what's the bottom line?"

Coworker: "I'm pretty sure the job will have to be done over. This will delay completion by about two weeks."

Manager: "So who will eat the cost?"

Coworker: "I'll have to hash this out with him. It's frustrating."

Manager: "I can imagine."

Coworker: "So now I'm not sure if we can trust this contractor going forward."

Manager: "Any other lessons for us?"

Coworker: "I think I need to keep a closer eye on these projects. I just trusted him to get it done right."

Manager: "What do you want to do?"

Coworker: "I'm going to have to look him in the eye and have a talk. I'll let you know how that goes."

Manager: "Sounds good."

Tips to optimize the way you guide learning:

- Be on the lookout for on-the-job experiential learning opportunities.

- When you ask open-ended questions, always let the other person do most of the talking. Your job is to listen to make sure you understand what the other person is telling you.

- Give a copy of the five reflection questions to your co-workers (Appendix 3, "The 5 Magic Reflection Questions"). Encourage them to record their answers in writing.

This chapter in a nutshell:

- **Successes and setbacks happen, but people don't automatically learn from them.**

- **Coaching people to learn from what happens at work is a powerful way to create smarter team members and improve their performance.**

- **You can make sure the learning actually happens by asking five open-ended questions that get at what happened, why, consequences, the lesson, and next steps.**

Learn more about facilitating learning from experience:

- Colin Beard and John P. Wilson, *Experiential Learning*, 4th Ed. (Kogan Page, 2018)

- Meredith Bell, *Strong for Performance* (First Summit Publishing, 2020)

"If what you are doing is not moving you towards your goals, then it's moving you away from your goals."

Brian Tracy

"One of the most important things a leader can do is lead by example. If you want everyone else to be passionate, committed, dedicated, and motivated, you go first."

Marshall Goldsmith

7

....

Get Buy-in for Expectations

Having clear expectations is a form of empowerment. How can people meet or exceed expectations if they don't know what these are? And how can you show appreciation or give constructive feedback if neither you nor the other person understands what's acceptable or outstanding?

Toward the end of Denny's career as an Army officer, he worked for a Navy captain who once commanded a submarine. He was easy to get along with, but Denny was never sure where he stood. There were lots of ways he could approach his job, but he wasn't sure how his boss defined outstanding performance. His commanding officer had never given him guidance about what he hoped to see.

One day Denny asked him if he was happy with his work so far. The answer he got did little to clarify his situation. The captain smiled and said, *"I'll know it when I see it. When you're doing great, I'll send you a note like this."* On a piece of paper he wrote two letters—"BZ"—and handed it to him. *"Bravo Zulu,"* he said. *"In the Navy, that means job well done."*

So working with the captain was a bit of a guessing game. Denny had no choice but to deliver what he assumed the captain would want, do a little extra now and then, and routinely thank the captain for his support. He got his share of BZs, but in retrospect he knows he probably could have accomplished a lot more in that assignment.

A team member's role is not always obvious. Maybe there's a clearly written job description, but it won't address specific projects or define high performance. And new challenges present themselves. What's needed in the workplace can change. The economy fluctuates regularly. When new team members arrive with their unique abilities, roles could change. Customer preferences could change. In the 21st century, the technologies that support performance are constantly changing. With artificial intelligence and robotics keeping pace with science fiction, many jobs could eventually be replaced by technology.

Appreciating each other's roles and giving meaningful feedback starts with having clearly understood expectations. It's not fruitful to get upset with someone's performance if they don't understand what it should be.

Also, team members will be far more enthusiastic about achieving expectations if they're involved in creating them. There are several ways to think about the role of team members in problem-solving, decision-making, and defining expectations:

- **Consultation.** If you know the team cares about what's supposed to happen, and if you have time to involve them, their participation to get agreement will create buy-in. Because they helped shape expectations, they'll "own" them and more enthusiastically work to achieve them.

- **Delegation.** When team members are heavily invested in the outcome, you trust their judgment, and you know you can live with any choice they make, then you can let them define expectations. Your role at that point would be to empower them as needed.

- **Autocratic decision.** Sometimes it's inappropriate to ask for input. When safety is involved, if it's a life-or-death situation, or if the action is critical and there's simply no time to discuss options, a leader must explain what has to be done and why. In addition, if team members have no concerns about the decision one way or the other, you can simply tell them what you want.

In the end, enthusiasm matters more than compliance. The key is not just establishing clear expectations, but when possible, going one step further: having expectations that people agree are fair and effective, so they not only understand what should happen, *they want to achieve it.* To get that kind of buy-in, expectations need to be created by getting the input of team members: mutually discussed, created and agreed-upon. In his book, *Straight-Line Leadership,* Dusan Djukich frames expectations as agreements:

> *"A straight-line leader manages commitments and agreements. He creates agreements with team members and enters into those agreements on an adult-to-adult basis. All communication is done with mutual respect. There is no giving in to the temptation to be intimidating, bossy, or all-knowing, which comes from having expectations and no courage to make an agreement."*

Recognize the "buy-in moment"

...when faced with a goal, milestone or task, and you expect specific effort or results from a coworker.

Engage your "buy-in mindset"

People are more motivated to accomplish a difficult objective if they own it, and so I ask for their input to help frame it.

Scenario #1:

Manager: "Your guys are taking too long to load deliveries. You know the trucks have to leave the bays by eight. Not nine. Yesterday some left at nine-thirty. I want you to pick up the pace."

Team Leader: "Most of them get out on time. But sometimes we get changes in the orders, and that causes delays."

Manager: "I don't care. The trucks aren't getting to the stores on time, and everything is backing up."

Team Leader: "I'm already pushing the guys pretty hard."

Manager: "Then push harder. Stores are complaining about late deliveries."

Team Leader: "It would help if the stores would get their input in faster."

Manager: "That's not our job. Our job is distribution. Just do your job and get the trucks on the road by eight."

Team Leader: "We'll do our best."

Scenario #2:

Manager: "We have a problem. Yesterday at nine there were still trucks at the bays."

Team Leader: "I know."

Manager: "So what's the problem? What can you do about it?"

Team Leader: "We don't have a problem when the store orders are ready to go. But sometimes they're late coming in, and sometimes there are changes. This holds things up."

Manager: "We've got to get the trucks on the road by eight or the stores will be restocking during peak shopping hours. That would be bad for the company. For all of us."

Team Leader: "I know. I think my guys understand that."

Manager: "So what can we do about it? If you had the power to change something, what would you do?"

Team Leader: "I think the store managers need to be reminded of the importance of getting orders in on time. And what happens when they don't."

Manager: "I can help get that message out. What can you do to improve the loading?"

Team Leader: "It would help if store managers understood that if final orders aren't in on time, either deliveries can't leave here by eight, or some of them may not be fulfilled."

Manager: "Yes, I can make that point. But what can you do?"

Team Leader: "I can talk with my crew. Maybe there's a more efficient approach to our loading. You know they feel good when they finish on time. So they may have ideas, something we haven't tried yet."

Manager: "That sounds like a plan. I'd like to know what you come up with. Maybe we can get this machine humming at top speed."

Team Leader: "Okay. Let me know what happens with the store managers, and I'll get back to you about our ideas."

Manager: "Excellent. Let's talk again tomorrow."

In the first scenario, the manager took an autocratic approach to deal with the performance issue. She's the one responsible for the distribution center, and she's the one getting heat from the stores. So she exercised her authority by issuing a directive. She reminded the team leader what's required and applied additional pressure to deliver. But it wasn't the kind of guidance that would inspire the best efforts of the people who do the work, and it failed to address the underlying issues that created the problem.

In the second scenario, the manager didn't just assume that workers need to try harder. Instead of simply taking a traditional command-and-control approach, she asked the team leader for input. She involved the team leader to explore and resolve the issue and set realistic expectations. This sent a message that she respects the team leader's experience and motivation. By involving the team leader in solving the problem, she created the possibility of making changes that could actually improve the situation. Because the team leader helped shape the expectations, he "bought in" to them.

The first scenario has a "we-they" feel to it. In the second, the team leader experiences the challenge as "we're in this together."

In short, there's an important difference between setting expectations and getting buy-in for them. If you're working with capable, experienced people who care about their work, and if you have time to consult with them, it's smart to get their input. Instead of simply giving orders, discuss what needs to happen. With their input, there's a greater chance that what's expected will be both ambitious and realistic—and that they'll be motivated to achieve it. When discussing what needs to happen, aim for an expectation that:

- Acknowledges and addresses issues

- Is targeted to achieve the mission, goal, or milestone

- Has a realistic chance for success

- Clarifies the support they need to achieve it

Clear expectations are the essential first step to later giving feedback about performance, whether it's appreciation for a job well done or constructive feedback when expectations aren't met. In the latter instance, a component of the feedback will be to reaffirm or reset the expectations (see Chapter 10, "Give Feedback Constructively"). If you can get buy-in for the effort and results you need, you'll have a greater chance of inspiring support and cooperation.

This chapter in a nutshell:

- **If you want people to live up to expectations, they need to know exactly what these are.**

- **Expectations can be ambitious, but they need to be realistic.**

- **When people are included in the process of setting or adjusting expectations, they "buy in," which elevates their desire to do what's required.**

Learn more about establishing expectations:

- Sam Kaner, *Facilitator's Guide to Participatory Decision-Making* (Jossey-Bass, 2014)

- Mel Silberman, *PeopleSmart* (Barrett-Koehler, 2000), Skill 3

- Dusan Djukich, *Straight-Line Leadership* (Robert D. Reed, 2011), Chapter 26

- John Maxwell, *The 21 Irrefutable Laws of Leadership* (Thomas Nelson, 2007), Chapter 14

"At times our own light goes out and is rekindled by a spark from another person. Each of us has cause to think with deep gratitude of those who have lighted the flame within us."

Albert Schweitzer

8

....

Offer Encouragement

People's knowledge, skills, values, attitudes and motivation can lead to high levels of achievement. Individuals may also bring a unique set of core strengths, such as patience, self-confidence, persistence, and many others. Such strengths can make them resilient, allowing them to continue giving their best effort in spite of the inevitable difficulties associated with any workplace challenge. Faced with a setback, people who believe in themselves and want to succeed eventually recover, take heart, and continue striving.

On the other hand, it's possible for people to become so disheartened that they give up. Imagine a gifted runner who, in the final stretch of a race, trips and falls. In pain, she realizes that much of her lead is lost. If she gets back up, she might still have a chance of winning. But will she recover?

Repeated setbacks can sometimes feel like that. Problems, disappointments, accidents, or failures can sometimes feel so devastating that a person "loses heart." The negatives can seem so overwhelming that a person loses sight of what's possible, feeling that continuing to strive isn't worth the effort.

This is what we call *discouragement*.

When self-encouragement doesn't kick in, others can help a person recover. Most people have the idea that offering encouragement is a no-brainer, that if you care about someone, encouragement comes naturally. However, helping a dispirited person is actually a special skill, and few people are practiced in it. What many folks think of as encouragement can have the opposite effect.

The classic form of mistaken encouragement is false assurance. "Everything is going to be all right." Has anyone ever said that to you? Even though they may have offered it with a kind spirit, statements like this are empty if they have no basis.

Another way people try to encourage is to sugar-coat reality. They may say, "This isn't so bad." Denying an unpleasant truth is a common coping mechanism, but anyone who's been brought to their knees by adversity knows that the situation really is this bad, and saying that it isn't doesn't help.

Some take the tough love approach, saying something like, "Come on, stuff happens. Get over it." When this does work, it's usually when particularly strong individuals are already encouraging themselves.

Discouragement happens when an adverse situation causes someone to be so focused on their pain and the negatives that they're no longer acknowledging the positives of their situation—even though the upsides are real and valid. For encouragement to work, the key is to be reality-based. Every situation is a mixture of negative and positive elements: challenges and opportunities; problems and solutions; advantages and disadvantages; mistakes and lessons learned.

As with any communication skill, the first step is to notice when someone is discouraged and approach them with the right attitude.

Recognize the "encouragement moment"

...when you notice that something has happened to cause a coworker to be discouraged.

Engage your "encouragement mindset"

People sometimes don't bounce back from adversity right away. I remind them of their strengths, what's possible, and that their coworkers want to support them.

The job of an encourager is to help restore a balanced perspective—one that reminds the individual about the good in a bad situation. You can use these elements of encouragement in sequence, in any order, or in isolation:

- **Listen with empathy to understand.**

- **Affirm a person's strengths.**

- **Restore perspective.**

- **Offer support.**

Listen with empathy to understand.

Listening is first on this list because when you listen, you find out what happened to cause what your coworker is feeling. Even though you might be tempted to rescue someone who is temporarily derailed, listening is not about telling the individual what they should be thinking, feeling and doing. By listening, we mean what we described in Chapter 4 ("Listen to Understand"): focusing your attention, sensing their feelings, listening for the meaning, and checking what you hear.

If you're listening well, a discouraged individual may start "venting." You might hear frustration and anger. This is a good sign. When someone expresses negative feelings, it's because they need to. Typically, they'll feel relieved afterward. Sometimes this is all they need to "snap out of it."

Affirm a person's strengths.

Nobody is perfect; everyone is a unique blend of strengths and weaknesses. The idea is to remind the person of their strengths. When things go wrong, people sometimes feel guilt and blame themselves. They may feel inadequate. They may experience a blow to their self-esteem and self-confidence. They can temporarily lose sight of who they are and what they're capable of.

When someone focuses on their shortcomings, they need to be reminded of their strengths. Your coworker will probably be focused on the failure at hand, not past achievements, so it can help to bring up examples of where they've succeeded before in equally tough or even tougher situations.

Restore perspective.

In addition to an unbalanced view of themselves, a discouraged individual may also focus on the negatives in their situation. That's natural—these are the issues that are causing distress.

To restore a balanced, realistic perspective, first acknowledge the negatives. Then remind the person that the situation isn't all bad. There are advantages, potentials, opportunities, resources and other upsides. Pointing out the positives is helpful, because they're real, too.

Offer support.

When someone has been discouraged by difficulty or failure, they may wonder where they stand. Do you still believe in their ability to succeed? In light of current setbacks, will you withdraw your support? Now is the time to reassure them that you're still very much in their corner.

Let's take a look at an example of effective encouragement. Notice how Coworker 1 senses that Coworker 2 needs encouragement and then applies all the elements:

Coworker 1: "Hey..."

Coworker 2: "Mmm..."

Coworker 1: "You don't seem your usual bigger-than-life self today."

Coworker 2: "Smaller-than-life is more like it."

Coworker 1: "That doesn't sound good. What's up?"

Coworker 2: "You know the third-quarter projections that are due Friday?"

Coworker 1: "Sure."

Coworker 2: "Well I just realized I've been working off of last year's data. My report is useless."

Coworker 1: "So you're back at square one."

Coworker 2: "Right. Along with a big hunk of my life for the past month."

Coworker 1: "You put an awful lot into it."

Coworker 2: "I really did. And for nothing."

Coworker 1: "No wonder you're bummed out. Sorry, dude."

Coworker 2: "Yeah. It's my fault for not paying attention. I feel like a total fool."

Coworker 1: "No way. Anybody could have made that mistake. You're a smart guy, and now you're even smarter."

Coworker 2: "Ha. Maybe so. But where does that leave me?"

Coworker 1: "Well, for starters, I bet you learned a lot working on the project. Based on your experience, I wonder if you know a more efficient way to input the data."

Coworker 2: "What do you mean?"

Coworker 1: "You now know what goes where, so instead of doing it piecemeal, why not get Jennifer to write you a simple program to draw in the data?"

Coworker 2: "You think she can do that?"

Coworker 1: "She did a little job like that for me not long ago, and it only took a couple hours. I'm sure she'd be willing to help out."

Coworker 2: "You know, that's worth considering. I'll talk to her about it."

Coworker 1: "You could still have the report done by Friday."

Coworker 2: "Maybe. Thanks for the tip."

Coworker 1: "You bet. Let me know if I can help."

Coworker 2: "I will."

Coworker 1: "And hey....You da man!"

Coworker 2: "Ha! Thanks."

What Coworker 1 does first is listen and empathize. Then she helps Coworker 2 recover a balanced, realistic perspective of himself and his situation. It's remarkable how people recover with genuine encouragement.

Tips for encouraging someone:

- **Help the person visualize a positive outcome.** When someone is especially discouraged, try asking a question such as, "If you were to imagine this situation turning out really well, what would that look like?" It's nearly impossible to answer this question without seeing things that could help turn a situation around.

- **Know when to stop encouraging.** While listening, if you sense that the person is beginning to take heart, let them go the rest of the distance without your help. Remember it's always better if someone thinks, *I did this myself.* If you listen well, it's possible that none of the other strategies will be needed. Aim to deliver just the right amount of encouragement to someone who needs it.

- **Don't wait for discouragement to offer encouragement.** From time to time, offer bits of encouragement while your coworker is still doing well. Express your appreciation and belief in their abilities. This will help keep them feeling confident, so that when the inevitable problems and frustrations happen, their discouragement will be minimal or non-existent. With this kind of "inoculation," a person can stay strong enough to encourage themselves.

To get your "reps," stay alert for encouragement moments, such as when a coworker:

- Experiences a setback

- Doesn't receive the support they need

- Is criticized

- Tries to fix a problem, and it doesn't work

- Has difficult problems at home

This chapter in a nutshell:

- **Discouragement is a real possibility in a challenging work environment.**

- **Not everyone recovers from adversity quickly.**

- **You can encourage by reminding people of their strengths, what's possible, and your willingness to be there with support.**

Learn more about encouragement:

- Larry Crabb, *Encouragement: The Unexpected Power of Building Others Up* (Zondervan, 2013)

- Mark Goulston, M.D., *Just Listen* (AMACOM, 2015), Chapter 17

- Dusan Djukich, *Straight-Line Leadership* (Robert D. Reed, 2011), Chapter 28

"Nothing else can quite substitute for a few well-chosen, well-timed, sincere words of praise. They're absolutely free and worth a fortune."

Sam Walton

"Feeling gratitude and not expressing it is like wrapping a present and not giving it."

William Arthur Ward

9

....

Express Appreciation

It isn't easy to get people to do their best work. They might have superior knowledge of the business, the right skills, a lot of experience, and the support of others to achieve at a high level. The question is, do they want to put that much of themselves into their work?

From time to time, for reasons of their own, employees will do something outstanding. But what if no one seems to notice? What if managers or coworkers don't acknowledge the extra effort? Who could blame them for feeling unappreciated? They might be internally motivated to do what they're capable of doing and even recognize that achieving high levels of quality is more satisfying than just doing what's required. Or they might decide that giving that much of themselves isn't worth it, especially if their manager doesn't hesitate to point out when something goes wrong.

Managers *should* give constructive feedback when people are ignoring regulations, causing problems, or making a half-hearted effort. On the other hand, people sometimes feel their best efforts go unnoticed. They may perceive that they get a lot more criticism than praise. Often managers take the good for granted, focusing mostly on problems. The bottom line is that if people only hear criticism, they'll feel underappreciated for the good things they do, and they won't respond enthusiastically when you point out what you'd like them to change. This is unfortunate, because positive feedback is more motivating than negative feedback, even if it's constructive.

> *If you expect great things from people, you need to continuously build them up, not tear them down.*

The goal isn't to praise every little thing people do. They know when they've earned your genuine appreciation and when they haven't, when you're sincere and when you're just going through the motions. While it's true that most managers don't praise their team members often enough, it's usually because they're not in the habit of noticing legitimate opportunities. They seem to have no problem catching people doing things wrong; they need to make a more consistent effort to "catch them doing things right." It starts with making a practice of looking for opportunities.

Recognize the "appreciation moment"

...when you notice that someone has done something well, made a special effort, or achieved something outstanding.

Engage your "appreciation mindset"

I notice when people have done their best and affirm them for their effort.

A few years ago, Meredith posted an article about expressing appreciation on her blog. She received a heartfelt email afterwards from Wayne McEvilly, a gifted concert pianist:

> *"Your post brought to mind a fan letter I wrote to Dame Myra Hess, the great British pianist whose work was a*

service to her nation and to humanity. I told her that her music brought us closer to God. She wrote back (this astounded me since my praise was a drop in the ocean of praise she had experienced from royalty and the world at large) and said, 'You must never think that praise such as yours is not wanted, or needed.' Those words from 1957 still ring clear in my mind, and I remind myself never to allow sincere praise to be muted by any circumstance."

Wayne's note reminds us that *everyone* needs to be appreciated, no matter how much financial success, status or fame they've achieved in life.

A simple "Thank You!"

It's easy to neglect saying "Thanks!" because you may be in a hurry or focused on a pressing problem. The thing is, when people feel unappreciated for the good things they do, chances are they'll withhold that extra effort in the future. The recommendation is simple: when someone has helped you out, moved things forward, or done something excellent, don't let the moment pass. Express your genuine gratitude.

*"Jill, **thank you** for reminding me to take the ORCAN file to the meeting. I would have been sitting there fat, dumb, and not so happy."*

*"Harry, **thank you** for taking over the phones today. I know it's not your job, but Chuck had to leave early, and you handled every conversation in a calm, friendly way."*

You get the idea. It's really simple. Just be someone who remembers to say *thanks*. An email is fine, but when gratitude is expressed face-to-face with genuine, heartfelt appreciation, it's even more effective.

Positive Feedback

Recognition. Affirmation. Gratitude. Appreciation. Praise. Positive strokes. Pats on the back. Attagirls. Attaboys. All good stuff! It's amazing how motivating a compliment can be. Any kind of acknowledgement of something done well will probably make someone feel good. And there's a simple way to make sure your positive feedback has maximum impact: instead of giving a general comment, *describe the specific action that pleased you—and share how you feel about it.*

Situation: A coworker gets a "Thank you!" and a smile from a customer.

General feedback: *"Good job, Joe!"* Or the manager could have offered a wink and a thumbs-up sign. No harm done. General praise is positive input, so it feels good. At least Joe knows his manager is happy. But when praise is specific, it has double the power.

Specific feedback: *"I saw that you didn't just recommend the standard fix. You asked the right questions and checked the database and found a better solution in the stockroom. It cost more, but the customer was thrilled. I love that you made the extra effort."*

Notice that Joe's manager owned the feedback. By using "I" and being specific about what Joe did, Joe knows exactly what was appreciated.

Situation: Manuel had to leave early, and at the end of the day, without being asked to do so, Hanna cleaned his workspace for him.

General feedback: *"You're a real team player!"* Nice! Who wouldn't like to hear that? Praise has even more impact when you tell a person how something they did made a difference.

Specific feedback: *"Hanna, I really appreciate that you took care of cleaning up after Manuel. He had to leave early, and otherwise it would have been on me to clean up. You saved me a lot of time."*

Appreciating Appreciation

This chapter has been about expressing appreciation. But when you're on the receiving end, it's just as important to do a good job of receiving it. If you're lucky, at some point someone will tell you how much they appreciate something you've done. When it happens, we hope it feels good!

However, if you want those positive strokes to come your way more often, *you want the person praising you to feel good about making you feel good*. When they express their appreciation, you don't want them to think they made a mistake. You want them to feel that their positive feedback was appreciated.

We mention this because many people, for a variety of reasons, feel awkward about responding to praise. It's possible they didn't think their effort was worth being singled out, that it was something they do all the time—no big deal. Sometimes people who don't have strong self-esteem distrust positive input from others. Or maybe an individual isn't used to receiving praise; it takes them by surprise, and they don't know what to say.

However, keep in mind that the person expressing appreciation almost always offers it with a good heart, with the expectation that it will be well received. So if you enjoyed the affirmation and hope it happens again someday, the solution doesn't involve some new technique brought to you by the experts of emotional intelligence. Your momma gave it to you back when she was teaching you to tie your shoes. She told you to remember to say "you're welcome" when someone says "thank you." It's the gracious thing to do.

An effective response to appreciation can simply be a version of your mother's advice, offered with sincerity and a smile:

"Thank you, it's nice to be appreciated."

"I'm glad you liked it."

"It's nice to know it helped."

"I appreciate that."

"Your feedback means a lot."

The key is to make sure you don't let the opportunity pass you by. Even if you feel a little embarrassed by praise, always express your appreciation for being appreciated. You'll be encouraging positive feedback. The workplace needs more of it!

Tips for making positive feedback more effective:

- **Commit to offering positive feedback more often than you give constructive feedback.** This may mean establishing a new habit: catching your coworkers doing things right. You already notice when things displease you; your discomfort signals you nearly every time. Noticing effort and achievement is a different experience. You'll need to raise your awareness by looking for those moments and then make a point of speaking up and sharing what you observed. Experts recommend praising others two or three times as often as you give constructive feedback.

- **Give positive feedback only when they've earned it.** Piling on the praise isn't always better. You might get away with expressing unearned praise once, but your coworkers will quickly catch on, and this kind of praise can backfire. If people sense you're insincere, they might question your motives and discount your praise even when it is sincere.

- **Praise a strong effort, even if it fails.** When an outstanding effort doesn't lead to success, there's a danger that people will beat themselves up about it. But that level of effort may well achieve success in the future. If you hope to see it repeated, let them know you appreciate their work! For example: *"I thought your briefing was outstanding. It was logical and your emphasis on versatility was compelling. The thing is, we don't always know what causes someone to say yes or no to our offer. We may think we know what their real needs are, but sometimes they haven't shared details that would make a difference in our approach. Your presentation would have worked wonders with most customers."*

- **Let them know you appreciate who they are.** People who have strong self-esteem and self-confidence are more likely to perform at high levels. Others are more self-critical. They have talents and strengths, but they rarely acknowledge them. So let people know you appreciate their value by spending time with them, asking about their work and life, listening deeply, and pointing out *specifically* the best aspects of who they are. For example: *"It means a lot to me that you always tell me the truth."* Avoid generalities such as, *"You're really smart,"* which don't communicate the potential of an individual to continue learning and growing.

- **Do it with feeling.** Let the individual know you really mean it. If you genuinely feel gratitude and appreciation, let your facial expressions, tone of voice, and nonverbal gestures communicate it.

- **Consider delivering recognition in private.** Yes, awards and honors are traditionally given in a brief ceremony in front of a group of coworkers or in a written announcement. Theoretically, it can mean more to the recipient when everyone is made aware of the achievement. In reality, this kind of display can embarrass the person being honored, and some observers may feel jealous or wonder if the ceremony is really to make the organization look good. So give some thought to whether public or private recognition makes sense in a given situation. What matters most is the sincerity with which the honor is given.

This chapter in a nutshell:

- **The goal of appreciation is to build people up, so they're motivated and confident about doing something outstanding.**

- **Most managers tend to give corrective feedback more often than they express appreciation.**

- **Positive feedback is a much stronger motivator than negative feedback, and it should be given more often than negative feedback.**

- **Managers need to get good at "catching people doing things right."**

- **The key to high-impact praise is to be specific about what they did and how you feel about it.**

- **In addition to affirming achievement and success, show appreciation for outstanding effort, even when it doesn't achieve the hoped-for results.**

- **Let people know you understand and appreciate their value.**

Learn more about expressing praise and appreciation:

- Ken Blanchard and Spencer Johnson, *The New One Minute Manager* (William Morrow, 2015)

- Marshall Goldsmith, *What Got You Here Won't Get You There* (Hyperion, 2007), Chapter 10

- David Rock, *Quiet Leadership* (HarperBusiness, 2007), Part Two, Step 1

"We all need people who will give us feedback. That's how we improve."

Bill Gates

10

....

Give Feedback Constructively

Whether you're a manager or a member of a work group, success depends on the people around you doing their best to contribute in their assigned roles. Yet people sometimes disappoint. They forget, they get distracted, they lose sight of what's needed from them—there are dozens of possible reasons for not measuring up.

When this happens, you need to bring the problem to their attention. If you don't, the shortfall in performance might continue. It's important, though, to avoid communicating your concern in a harsh way, especially if you're angry. That approach can wear people down instead of encouraging them to do better.

A typical critical reaction is to express irritation. This can take many forms: sarcasm, put-downs, name-calling, threats, commands, lectures, toxic questions, etc.

Denny has a vivid memory of a commanding officer who verbally reprimanded him. Denny's task that day was to escort a four-star general who was visiting a field training exercise. Denny was instructed to take the general by helicopter to visit two specific exercises. On the way to the second visit the general said, *"Tell the pilot to go to the marksmanship range instead."* Denny complied, and the general was pleased. But after the general left, his boss shouted his displeasure. *"I told you to take him to Areas 4 and 5, not the range. Can't you follow a simple order?"* Poking his finger into Denny's chest, he added, *"When I tell you to do something, damn it, you do it. You understand me?"*

The memory is vivid because Denny resented being treated this way. His mission was to help the visiting general see what he needed to see; the request was reasonable and he made it happen. His commanding officer should have been happy that he acted quickly to make the change and that the general was delighted with his visit. Instead, he was treated with contempt. Feeling that it was time to leave this kind of leadership behind, that afternoon Denny submitted his retirement papers.

When there are problems and issues, the shortfalls need to be brought to people's attention and dealt with in a constructive way. To inspire people to give their best effort, feedback needs to be encouraging.

Have you ever read *Anne Frank: The Diary of a Young Girl?* This classic is the account of a middle-school-age Jewish girl whose family was forced to hide from Nazi German soldiers who had conquered Holland during World War II. She survived long enough to leave behind her remarkable diary, though her life ended tragically in a concentration camp.

Not many readers have noticed that a major theme of her journal entries was her complaints about how the adults around her gave her feedback. *"If I talk, everyone thinks I'm showing off, when I'm silent they think I'm ridiculous, rude if I answer, sly if I get a good idea, lazy if I'm tired, selfish if I eat a mouthful more than I should, stupid, cowardly, crafty, etc. The whole day long I hear nothing else but that I am an insufferable baby, and although I laugh about it and pretend not to take any notice, I do mind."*

Of course, her family was in a uniquely stressful situation, and emotions often ran high. But still, as a consequence of how she was criticized, Anne distanced herself from her parents, especially her mother. One night her mother offered to say prayers with her, and Anne refused. *"I felt sorry for Mummy, very, very sorry, because I had seen for the first time in my life that she minds my coldness. I saw the look of sorrow on her face when she spoke of love not being forced. It is hard to speak the truth, and yet it is the truth: she herself has pushed me away, her tactless remarks and her crude jokes, which I don't find at all funny, have now made me insensitive to any love from her side."*

Even normally considerate and supportive coworkers can feel irritation and anger rising. Anyone frustrated by someone's subpar performance can react instinctively with a hurtful remark.

"What's wrong with you?"

"I can't believe you did that."

"What did you think you were doing?"

"How many times do I have to tell you…?"

"That was dumb, you know that?"

"Why did you do that?"

"Weren't you paying attention?"

"If you can't handle this, I'll find someone else."

"Sometimes I don't know what to do with you."

"Why don't you just do what you're told?"

People need feedback. They need to be told what they're doing well so they'll know to do it more often. They need to know when their behavior is causing problems, so they can make an effort to change. At the same time, the spirit of workplace feedback needs to be positive, so coworkers want to contribute to the team effort and grow stronger in their roles. Feedback needs to build people up, not tear them down. It needs to be communicated in such a way that the recipient perceives it as a gift.

To be effective, feedback needs to be delivered in an encouraging way that inspires resilience.

As with any communication skill, the first thing you need to do is be aware of when it's needed and approach it with the right attitude.

Recognize the "feedback moment"

...when a coworker's performance has come up short and you want to inspire them to do better.

Engage your "feedback mindset"

When I'm not happy with someone's behavior, I share how I feel about it in a positive, encouraging way.

I-Messages

In his book, *L.E.T.—Leader Effectiveness Training,* Thomas Gordon refers to a powerful technique he calls the "I-Message." The I-message is simply a phrase in which you use the pronoun "I" to own your feedback. For example, you might say, *"I'm disappointed that you've only made three follow-up calls this week."* Saying it this way is powerful because it states two things that can't be argued:

- What you specifically observed about the person's behavior

- How you feel about it

Implied in this I-message is an *expectation*, a standard of behavior previously agreed upon between managers and coworkers. For example: *"Based on what we discussed and agreed to, from now on you'll make at least 10 follow-up calls every day. Can I count on you to do that?"*

When you communicate an expectation this way, it sets up the possibility for future feedback, after you've observed the individual in action. Later, you can share *constructive feedback* when the agreed-upon behavior isn't met. Or you can share *positive feedback* when you've noticed this person making an effort. I-messages are important elements in both positive and constructive feedback, the goal of which should always be to encourage future success.

Constructive Feedback

People sometimes make mistakes, or for a variety of reasons their work is subpar. To get them to achieve what's been agreed to, you need to bring the issue to their attention. And you need to do it in a way that builds them up rather than tears them down.

In this example, the store manager complains to a mechanic, who is installing new tires:

Manager: "Hey, haven't I told you about recycling discarded packaging?"

Mechanic: "I guess so."

Manager: "And used parts?"

Mechanic: "Yeah, so?"

Manager: "Well, I found all this stuff in the trash can."

Mechanic: *No reply.*

Manager: "Listen, we recycle this stuff because it's good for business, so get that through your head."

Without realizing its impact, the manager implies that the mechanic is careless and doesn't have the best interests of the business in mind. Still, it's important to hold up a mirror to problem behavior, because people aren't always conscious when they aren't doing what's expected. And if there are serious consequences, you need to help them get back on track while holding them accountable.

Fortunately, it's possible to point out issues in a way that anyone will accept. During the past several decades, experts in interpersonal communication have developed a well-tested approach to giving constructive feedback that gets the job done while encouraging rather than criticizing and offending. The approach involves five steps:

1. **Affirm the good.**

2. **Describe *specifically* the problem behavior.**

3. **Explain its impact.**

4. **Reset expectations.**

5. **Encourage and offer support.**

Step 1: Affirm the good.

You don't want to sugar-coat or downplay your feedback; but if you only mention the unwanted behavior, it will make a person think you don't notice the good things they've done. If your feedback only mentions the negatives, they'll think you're being unfair and may discount the rest of what you say. They may even argue with you. To defuse their defensiveness, before you start talking about what bothers you, mention at least one thing related to the actions at hand that you appreciate. For example:

"Ted, I know that most of the time you're really thoughtful about what you say to customers, and I really appreciate that."

Step 2: Describe *specifically* the problem behavior.

A behavior isn't the same as values, attitudes, opinions or feelings. A behavior is something you can observe. So describe precisely what the person did—and only what they did. Put the description in context: how it violated an agreement, norms, or values. Do this without emotion and without making assumptions about intentions. Here's an example of a specific behavior description:

> *"I overheard how you handled that customer's complaint. You interrupted her three times so she couldn't finish explaining her issue, and your tone of voice sounded impatient."*

Step 3: Explain its impact.

Describe the consequences of the behavior, even—if appropriate—your feelings about it, such as surprise, concern, disappointment, etc.

> *"She left without getting her problem resolved, and she seemed upset. I'm concerned we may have lost her business and she'll tell others about her experience."*

At this point, your coworker may try to explain. *This is an important "listening moment,"* so be prepared to engage your "listen to understand" skills. Anything else could cause a rational conversation to escalate to an emotional one.

Ted: "She came in making demands, and her sarcasm put me off."

You: "You didn't like the way she talked to you, and it affected how you dealt with her."

Ted: "Yeah. I probably didn't do a good job of finding out what her problem was."

You: "You're usually a very good listener and problem solver, but it seemed as if you momentarily forgot to make an effort."

Ted: "I guess so."

Step 4: Reset expectations.

Ask for the behavior you want, and explain why. If the action had a serious consequence, discuss ways to make amends. This will create a path for the person to "make things right again." Get agreement on future behavior (see Chapter 7, "Get Buy-in for Expectations"); if you sense they aren't sure what's expected, you can make suggestions. If the problem they caused wasn't that serious, simply conclude by reaffirming the desired behavior.

You: "Ted, you know our business is all about service, and we're trying to earn a reputation of being the best in town. Actually, you're very good at turning complaints into solutions. I've seen you do it so many times."

Ted: "I blew it this time. I guess she caught me off guard. But that's no excuse. A customer's attitude shouldn't keep me from meeting their needs. It won't happen again. I have her phone number. I think I'll call her to apologize and try to make it right with her."

Step 5: Encourage and offer support.

Always sandwich the meat of constructive feedback between two positives. In addition to the affirmation in Step 1, conclude your feedback by expressing confidence in the person's ability to deliver, and confirm your support.

"That would be great. I appreciate all you do, your positive attitude, and your willingness to learn from this. If you need something from me to make her happy, let me know."

Tips for making constructive feedback more encouraging:

- **Calm down first.** When you're upset with someone's behavior, you can avoid saying something emotional, aggressive, or sarcastic by simply saying nothing while you let your emotions subside. Your goal is to encourage someone to behave differently, not to vent or create defensiveness or resentment. If you say something hurtful, they won't believe you mean well.

- **Don't hold it inside.** Giving constructive feedback is never easy, and for this reason people sometimes decide not to say anything. But if you need someone to make more of an effort, don't put off bringing it up. If you let your discontent stew, eventually you'll need to address so many instances that happened in the past that the person won't be able to deal with all of it. And chances are you'll feel the need to express feelings that have mounted up over time.

- **Only address issues the person can do something about.** Sometimes the thing that displeases you is beyond the other person's ability to fix, so confronting them with it will be pointless and unfair.

- **Be sure of your facts.** Otherwise, the focus of your feedback could be in error, in which case it will be discounted. The best approach is to stick to behavior you've observed personally.

- **Focus on only one issue at a time.** Feedback is successful if the other person later makes an effort to change behavior. Addressing more than one issue at a time can be more than most people can handle.

- **Think about what you'll say.** Before you speak, take a moment to remember the five basic elements of constructive feedback. Mentally rehearse, so you say the most effective things in the most effective sequence.

- **Give feedback while the incident is still fresh (within 24 hours).** If you don't address the issue in a timely manner, your coworker may not remember exactly what happened and may wonder why you waited so long to bring it up.

- **Keep your feedback private and confidential.** Respect the needs and feelings of the individual. If you embarrass someone in front of others, you'll create resentment, which will diminish their motivation to change and negatively impact your relationship.

- **Check that the person is ready to receive feedback.** Ask if this is a good time to share feedback. For a variety of reasons, the individual may not be ready to consider what you have to say. If so, you can say, "That's fine. We can talk about it later."

- **Deliver constructive feedback face-to-face.** Not in an email or text message or on the phone.

- **Mention specific actions and behaviors.** If you talk about actions you've observed, it's hard for the person to deny or challenge you. So don't mention values, attitudes, personality or other factors which you can't observe directly.

- **If the individual responds, listen to understand.** You may learn more about the circumstances, which could affect how you frame your expectations.

- **Be honest.** Tell it like it is. Don't sugar-coat your description of the behavior, even if delivering it makes you feel uncomfortable.

- **Be sincere.** Don't just say the words as if they were part of a formula. Talk about what you actually saw and how you really felt about it.

- **Own your feedback—use "I-statements."** If the behavior displeases you, say so. Don't say, "The team isn't going to like it."

This chapter in a nutshell:

- **The purpose of constructive feedback is to tell people about their problem behavior in an encouraging way, so you build them up instead of tear them down.**

- **Constructive feedback should be positive. Sandwich your feedback with an affirmation on the front end and encouragement at the end.**

- **Using I-statements, your feedback should acknowledge the good they do, describe the person's problem behavior specifically, reveal the impact it had on you and others, reset the behavior you need, and offer encouragement and support.**

- **Be accurate, sincere, thoughtful, and respectful when giving feedback.**

Learn more about giving constructive feedback:

- Rick Maurer, *Feedback Toolkit* (Productivity Press, 1994)

- Marshall Goldsmith, *What Got You Here Won't Get You There* (Hyperion, 2007), Chapter 6

"Feedback is the breakfast of champions."

Rick Tate

"Treat every piece of advice as a gift."

Marshall Goldsmith

11

....

Accept Feedback Graciously

Chapter 10 ("Give Feedback Constructively") affirmed the value of constructive feedback and how to deliver it effectively. In this chapter, we reverse the situation and focus on how to respond when *you're* the one receiving the feedback.

Even if someone's feedback is poorly communicated—for example, criticism—it's still worth its weight in gold, if you accept it with an open mind and a gracious spirit. The reason is simple: no one is perfect, and most people have blind spots. You may not see yourself the way others see you, and you could be doing things that are detrimental to team success and your own career.

If you're like most people, you learned to communicate "on the street," so to speak. You acquired your way of interacting not from formal instruction and professional coaching, but from family and friends. So it's possible that some people are put off by one or more of your habitual ways of relating to them. It could be anything:

- Failure to keep people informed of your work

- Formal, distancing demeanor

- Habit of expressing impatience with others

- Failure to offer needed support

- Lack of interest in who they are and their personal lives

The consequence of unintended slights or dysfunctional behavior can result in a loss of trust, loyalty, and motivation. You could become a weak link on your own team, holding them back from higher levels of performance or even accomplishing the team mission.

Feedback can hold a mirror to your behavior, informing you about problems and issues you weren't aware of, empowering you to do something about it. Most people are reluctant to offer feedback, because they aren't sure how to phrase it in the best way, and they aren't sure how it will be received. This is why you should consider any feedback you get as "a gift."

An important question: *If you're lucky enough to get some constructive feedback, what are the chances it will be offered again in the future?*

The answer is simple: 100%—*if you accept the feedback graciously.*

Recognize the "accept feedback graciously moment"

...when someone has given you feedback and you want to encourage this kind of input in the future.

Engage your "accept feedback graciously mindset"

I ask for feedback, and when someone gifts me with it in any form, I listen without reacting, thank them, and follow up with an effort to change my behavior.

The purpose of this chapter is to outline what experts have said about accepting feedback in a way that reassures the people who gave it that it was received in the best possible way. Here are five things you can do that will assure people that you're genuinely open to receiving feedback:

- **Ask for feedback.**

- **Listen without being defensive.**

- **Apologize.**

- **Thank them for their feedback.**

- **Follow up.**

Ask for feedback.

Typically, feedback is given unsolicited. Or it could be given as a part of a 360-degree feedback project.

But what if you didn't wait to be surprised with it? What if you proactively asked for it?

"As we try to tackle the big changes coming up, it's important that you're getting the support you need from me. All of you work hard, and I sense I could probably be more supportive, so I'd like your feedback. What am I doing that could be holding us back? How can I be more supportive? Please give me your honest opinions. I promise to take them seriously."

Imagine the impact this would have on their perceptions of your openness to feedback.

Listen without being defensive.

Most people feel blindsided by feedback. This causes them to make a classic mistake: they try to defend themselves. This is a natural emotional reaction. Criticism—or even well-stated constructive feedback—never feels good. In fact, it can feel as though you've been attacked. And if you feel your hard work goes unappreciated most of the time, the feedback may even seem unfair. The tendency is to stand up for yourself, justify your behavior, and deflect or even deny the input.

If you respond with defensiveness, though, you'll send the message that their feedback wasn't accepted, that it was futile. Put yourself in their shoes. Given that offering feedback is risky for them, do these two things to ensure that you receive more of this kind of helpful input in the future:

- **Suppress your defensiveness.** Whenever you receive any kind of feedback, the most important thing you can do is listen to what the person is saying without trying to justify your behavior. Think of this as an absolute rule. Defensiveness will damage your ability to internalize the feedback and discourage feedback in the future.

- **Listen to understand.** Do this instead of getting defensive. Focus your attention and listen without speaking until you think you know what they're trying to say. Then check the message (see Chapter 4, "Listen to Understand"). In the process, you can identify specifically what they'd like to see more of.

Apologize.

Don't think of this as a mandatory step. But if the feedback you're getting reveals that you've caused an issue, it can be a powerful element of your reaction. Executive coach Marshall Goldsmith says this about accepting feedback graciously: "I regard apologizing as the most magical, healing, restorative gesture human beings can make." Many people feel that owning up to a mistake will damage how they're perceived. Actually, the opposite is true: people are already aware of your issue and an apology communicates that you recognize it and genuinely want to make amends.

Thank them for their feedback.

Feedback is a gift. This isn't a cute woo-woo notion. Feedback can tell you things about yourself that you weren't aware of, things that can help you be more successful. And this high-value offering will be given to you by people who aren't sure how to say it or even that you'll appreciate receiving it. There are lots of ways to say "Thank you." The key is to say it in a completely genuine way. Make sure people know you mean it, and tell them what you plan to do about it.

Feedback giver: "I've got something I need to tell you. Is this a good time?"

You: "Sure."

Feedback giver: "We're having a hard time setting priorities. This past week different people have received conflicting messages from you. They aren't consistent. We're not sure what we're supposed to do."

You: "Can you tell me more? Some specifics?"

Feedback giver: "Okay. Bud says you told him we had to go final by COB Friday. You told me we had until next Tuesday. Jan said to include travel expenses, but I had the impression we wouldn't include those. So there's some confusion."

You: "It sounds like I haven't been clear about my guidelines."

Feedback giver: "Right."

You: "I appreciate your getting back to me about this. I'm sorry I caused all this confusion. I'll get these details corrected today by email, and I'll do my best to keep everyone on the same page."

Feedback giver: "Great."

You: "And thanks again for making me aware of this."

Feedback giver: "No problem."

Follow up.

If you accepted your feedback graciously, you'll need to follow through on your promises. If you committed to correct an issue or demonstrate a new behavior pattern, now you need to deliver.

Also, along the way you can ask for more feedback. Or even better, ask for what Marshall Goldsmith calls "feedforward." If this term is new to you, think of feedforward as getting input related to future behavior, while feedback is related to what happened in the past. All you need to do is ask for suggestions to improve an aspect of your behavior. For example:

"Lately, I've been trying to keep the team better informed. Would you please suggest at least two ways I can improve how I do that?"

Suppressing your defensiveness, listening to understand, apologizing, and expressing gratitude, then later asking for feedforward—these aren't typical reactions to feedback. They represent a significant paradigm shift from what people normally experience at work. It may be difficult for you to put this new approach into practice; but if you want people to continue giving you the gift of feedback, it's important for you to convey to them that it's worth the effort.

This chapter in a nutshell:

- **Most people react defensively to constructive feedback.**

- **Doing so will discourage people from sharing honest feedback with you.**

- **Accepting feedback graciously will convince people it was worth the effort.**

- **The paradigm shift: suppress defensiveness, listen to understand, apologize, express gratitude, follow through, and ask for feedforward.**

Learn more about accepting feedback:

- Marshall Goldsmith, *What Got You Here Won't Get You There* (Hyperion, 2007), Chapters 7, 11, and 12

- Meredith Bell, *Strong for Performance* (First Summit Publishing, 2020)

- Joe Folkman, *Turning Feedback into Change* (Novations, 1996)

- Harriet Lerner, *Why Won't You Apologize?: Healing Big Betrayals and Everyday Hurts* (Gallery Books, 2017)

"You never really understand a person until you consider things from his point of view....until you climb into his skin and walk around in it."

Harper Lee

"When you talk, you are only repeating what you already know. But if you listen, you may learn something new."

Dalai Lama

12

....

Engage in Dialogue

Conflicts and disagreements are similar. Two people find that they are at odds with each other.

Conflicts are about action. They imply that someone wants something you consider unacceptable or that you want something another person considers unacceptable.

On the other hand, a disagreement is about opinions or beliefs. The difference may simply be that the two of you think differently about something.

One area of Denny's work is helping parents raise happy, successful independent adults. While speaking with parents, he has often found himself disagreeing with them about whether a teen should work to earn money. Many parents maintain that young people are too challenged to take on a part-time job. After school, they may have homework, sports, extracurricular activities, home chores, and, of course, friendships. These are all worthy activities, but they can create feelings of stress when kids try to do all of them well. Parents feel that a job would add to their teen's stress while diminishing their performance in school and other areas.

Denny believes that when young people earn their own money, they build self-reliance, responsibility, self-worth, and a strong work ethic—strengths that are important to success as an adult. In addition, kids can gain financial literacy. He reasons that giving teens money for what they want so they don't have to work can create a sense of entitlement. He believes adding a part-time job to their seemingly full plate will challenge them to manage their time better and reduce time-wasting activities. He points to stories about highly successful people who had to work when they were still in high school.

It's a difference of opinion that defies resolution. Both points of view are reasonable. In the best case, people engage in dialogue. They come to understand why other people think differently about the issue. They agree to disagree.

Disagreements can be uncomfortable. Questioning one of your long-held beliefs could mean questioning a whole set of related beliefs. Being confronted with an opposing opinion could make you feel defensive. Or you may sense that somebody's opinions could lead to trouble.

The way most people deal with a disagreement is to argue or debate—to prove that they're right. If you're like most people, you believe your point of view is better informed and based on more experience. And you may be right.

Manager: "I've decided to offer Randy the other team leader position. Just wanted to let you know."

Team leader: "But I recommended Sheryl. She has great leadership potential. Randy's not a leader."

Manager: "He deserves a shot. He's been here forever."

Team leader: "So has Jackson. You wouldn't promote Jackson, would you?"

Manager: "I think Randy will do fine."

Team leader: "You might lose Sheryl. She has such talent. She might take it somewhere else. She might think it's the good ol' boy network and the glass ceiling."

Manager: "I don't think so. She needs a little more time to learn the business."

Team leader: "She already knows more about our business than Randy does. She's action-oriented and has vision."

Manager: "Randy's no fool. He's practical. He'll stay the course."

Team leader: "You're making a big mistake."

Manager: "You're entitled to your opinion. But as you know, it's my call."

The manager and the team leader have different points of view on the issue of promotion, and neither one is convincing the other. This argument can only heat up until the manager plays the power card. She'll win the argument—technically, anyway. But her team leader is likely to:

- Resent losing an argument when he felt he was right

- Question the manager's judgment

- Passive-aggressively withdraw support for Randy to prove the manager wrong

- Feel wary about sharing his opinions in the future

This is why winning an argument can feel strangely like losing. Dialogue is a structured way of examining issues from different perspectives. Instead of defending your point of view, openly consider whether there may be more to an issue than you've already considered. Instead of arguing or debating, engage in a conversation simply to learn what the other person believes, and why—and to share your own thoughts on the subject.

When disagreeing with someone, share your thinking and then learn how they think without trying to prove you're right and they're wrong.

Recognize the "dialogue moment"

...when you realize that you don't agree with someone's point of view.

Engage your "dialogue mindset"

I may disagree with someone, but we're entitled to our opinions. Without trying to win an argument, I keep an open mind and make an effort to learn why the other person has this opinion.

The classic approach to dialogue has several elements:

1. **State your opinion.**
2. **Describe the facts and assumptions upon which your opinion is based.**
3. **Explain your reasoning.**
4. **Encourage the other person to examine your thinking.**
5. **Ask them to share their opinion, facts, assumptions, and reasoning.**

Step 1: State your opinion.

Initiate dialogue by acknowledging that your opinion is simply an opinion. The purpose of this all-important step is to set aside the message, "I know I'm right." Your opinions are important because they're the framework upon which you base many of your decisions. But opinions aren't final truths. Instead, they're always tentative conclusions based on available facts and assumptions. Since everyone doesn't share the same opinions, some may be founded on better facts and assumptions than others. Therefore, you stand to gain by considering the facts, assumptions, and conclusions of others.

"I see we don't agree on this. That's fine. Would you be open to our exchanging ideas about it? I don't want to argue or try to convince you I'm right. I'd just like to explain where I'm coming from and learn about your point of view. If it's okay with you, I'll go first. Here's my take...."

Step 2: Describe the facts and assumptions upon which your opinion is based.

Opinions aren't facts, but they're more valid if they're based on facts. However, a single fact doesn't necessarily make a strong case. Forming an opinion without considering enough factual evidence is called "jumping to conclusions."

"You see, I've always thought that...."

"And according to an article I read...."

"In my experience, I've observed that...."

"Once when I started my first business, several of my employees...."

Step 3: Explain your reasoning.

While personal feelings, instinct and intuition can guide your decision-making, it's important to ask whether your opinion makes sense. Is your opinion well supported by facts? Is your reasoning sound?

"So based on what these experts said and my experiences, I've concluded that most of the time...."

Step 4: Encourage the other person to examine your thinking.

To promote dialogue, ask the other person what he or she thinks about the assumptions, facts and reasoning you've shared. Again, listen to understand what's going on in the other person's mind. Resist the impulse to defend your opinions. Just give their evaluation consideration.

> *"That's where I'm coming from anyway. Do you have any thoughts about what I just said?"*

Step 5: Ask the other person to share their assumptions, facts, and reasoning.

Now it's the other person's turn to open up about their ideas— and time for you to listen. Are you willing to keep an open mind? Or are you so opposed to their take on the issue that you feel compelled to lecture or prove them wrong? Be prepared to listen simply to understand. If you feel defensiveness or other negative reactions, set them aside, so you can learn how the other person thinks.

Ask questions to discover the same three things you just shared:

1. **Their opinions.** Try to discover what they believe. If you hear something you didn't expect or something that conflicts with your own opinion, be careful not to get defensive.

   > *"Now that you know where I'm coming from, what are your thoughts?"*

2. **Facts and assumptions on which they base these opinions.** When you hear an opinion, ask how the person came to that opinion. If they offer evidence, ask if they have more. Take care that your tone of voice comes across as genuine curiosity, not as a challenge.

"I'm curious how you came to that conclusion. Was there something specific that you've read or heard?"

3. **Their reasoning.** As you listen, you may begin to understand their rationale. Summarize their reasoning to be sure you understand it.

"It sounds like you're saying this based on...and you've concluded that...."

It's equally effective to begin dialogue by first asking about the other person's point of view. As the individual explains their point of view, you should listen to the best of your ability.

The purpose of dialogue is not to expose the flaws in someone else's opinions or to teach them a better way of thinking. You engage in this kind of exchange to discover what the two of you believe—and why. That's all. Let the other person decide what to do with what you shared.

As for what they share, are you humble enough to consider the possibility of learning something new? During dialogue it's always possible to discover something you can use in your own thinking.

Only good things come from taking this approach. You begin to find out how their mind works, who they are. And they learn more about you, while discovering that it's not frustrating to be honest with you. They appreciate what opinions really are and the possibility of adopting more valid opinions. This is a far more valuable outcome than proving you're right and someone else is wrong.

Consider this example of the two people who disagree about an upcoming promotion:

Manager: "I've decided to offer Randy the other team leader position. Just wanted to let you know."

Team leader: "But I recommended Sheryl. I'm interested to know what led you to that decision."

149

Manager: "I know, but Randy has a ton of experience, and we owe it to him."

Team leader: "You believe experience is more important than leadership potential, and that loyalty is important. Why do you think that?"

Manager: "I've been around a long time, and in my opinion, experience in the business is worth its weight in gold. And without loyalty, you get resistance and discord."

Team leader: "But Sheryl is brilliant, a star. You've seen her leadership in action."

Manager: "True. I guess we disagree on this. So why do you think someone who's been here not quite a year should be promoted ahead of someone who's been here for eleven years?"

Team leader: "It's a leadership position, so I think the promotion should go to the individual who has demonstrated leadership. That's Sheryl, in my opinion, not Randy. What if it turns out that he's not so good at inspiring effort and teamwork?"

Manager: "I think he'll do fine."

Team leader: "So you feel that experience translates to effective leadership?"

Manager: "I do. It contributes to good business judgment. You know, in another firm, I was once promoted because I knew more about the business than anyone."

Team leader: "So based on your experience, you think it will also work out for Randy."

Manager: "I think so."

Team leader: "I get where you're coming from, but I'd ask you to give your decision a little more thought before you offer him the job."

Manager: "I have no problem with that."

Team leader: "And I'll give max support to the new team leader, whoever it may be."

Manager: "I know you will. I appreciate your willingness to consider my point of view. Your input is important to me."

Tips for optimizing the way you engage in dialogue:

- **Make a commitment to avoid arguments.** Disagreements are inevitable; they happen often and the instinct to react with authority is deeply ingrained. To sense the dialogue moment in time to avoid an argument will be tricky, and you'll have to make a concentrated effort.

- **Focus on the benefits.** Even if you feel you're right most of the time, you can learn a lot about your coworkers by sharing ideas without trying to prove you're right. Also, allowing them to consider your ideas in a non-argumentative way will demonstrate that you respect them and that you really do want to understand them. This is how dialogue can enrich workplace relationships.

To get your "reps," stay alert for dialogue moments like these:

- Somebody complains about something

- You disagree with something they say

- Your coworker expresses an opinion that's not consistent with your values

- Something someone said has surprised or shocked you

- Somebody says something that's inconsistent with facts

- Your coworker expresses an opinion that could lead to trouble

This chapter in a nutshell:

- **People may disagree, but arguments are counterproductive.**

- **The goal of dialogue is to avoid arguments and debates by learning about each other's thinking.**

- **To initiate dialogue, share your opinion, facts, assumptions, and reasoning.**

- **Then ask the other person about their opinion, facts, assumptions, and reasoning.**

- **Don't pursue dialogue to prevail over another person's opinion. Make it your goal to understand where they're coming from.**

Learn more about dialogue:

- William Isaacs, *Dialogue* (Random House, 2008)

- Marie-Eve Marchand, *The Spirit of Dialogue in a Digital Age* (Dialogue Publications, 2019)

"Unless both sides win, no agreement can be permanent."

Jimmy Carter

13

....

Resolve Conflict Creatively

When was the last time you were at odds with someone at work—when someone wanted to do something you considered unacceptable? You both felt justified in asking for what you wanted, but the conflict had the potential to damage your relationship.

There are many ways to resolve conflicts. Over the years, the most helpful reference we've found for understanding and using conflict resolution strategies is the Thomas-Kilmann model, designed by psychologists Kenneth Thomas and Ralph Kilmann. It compares five approaches, each combining two elements: "assertiveness" (trying to get what you want) with "cooperativeness" (trying to help the other person get what they want). Using the two elements (to a high or low degree) results in five different ways to resolve conflict, each with its own rationale, advantages, and disadvantages.

1. **Competing** (high assertiveness and low cooperativeness). In this approach, you seek a **win-lose** resolution. If you have the power to take this approach, you may get what you want, but at the expense of the other person, who fails to get what they want. The disadvantage to winning this way is that it can come to seem like losing, because it creates ill will and possibly drives the other person to seek other undesirable solutions. However, this

could be a necessary approach if it means protecting your rights or safety (or those of other people) or defending an all-important priority.

2. **Accommodating** (low assertiveness and high cooperativeness). This is considered a **lose-win** approach because instead of trying to get what you want, you give in to the wants of the other person. Accommodating could take the form of generosity or charity. Or you could give in if doing so promotes good will, and what you give up isn't that important to you. On the other hand, if sacrificing your own wants is your habit due to a desire to avoid conflict or constantly please others, you may build up resentment and other feelings that negatively impact your relationships as well as your self-esteem.

3. **Avoiding** (low assertiveness and low cooperativeness). This is the **lose-lose** approach. You simply refuse to deal with the conflict. Because neither party gets their needs met, this approach can allow the conflict to fester and gather intensity. On the other hand, avoiding the conflict can push resolving it into the future, if doing so avoids danger or if dealing with the issue later promises a better chance of success.

4. **Compromising** (moderate assertiveness and moderate cooperativeness). We consider this a **win/lose— win/lose** approach, because both parties get something but at the cost of giving up something they need. It's the "something is better than nothing" approach. It might mean splitting the difference, some give-and-take, or seeking a resolution in the middle ground. Partially satisfying both parties' needs may only temporarily resolve the conflict, because what has been given up will remain as an unsatisfied need.

5. **Collaborating** (high assertiveness and high cooperativeness). This is the **win-win** resolution—the opposite
of avoiding. When two people are in conflict, they back
off their initial demands and instead focus on their re-
spective needs. They then explore other possible solutions that promise to meet the needs of both. This approach requires mutual respect, a willingness to listen,
and creativity to find solutions.

While there may be situations where any of these approaches could be the most effective strategy, most of the time
our favorite is No. 5—*collaborating*. This option is a way for
both parties to the conflict to get their needs met, not by getting
their initial demands, but by exploring other solutions.

*The key is for both you and your coworker to back
off your initial wants and instead focus on the needs
that are driving the wants, and then creatively
search for other solutions that will address your
needs and your coworker's needs at the same time.*

The next time you're nose-to-nose with someone else, instead of giving in or relying on your authority to get your way,
consider the win-win approach. Calm your defensiveness, and
start with this:

Recognize the "conflict resolution moment"

*...when someone wants something you consider un-
acceptable or you want something another person
considers unacceptable.*

Engage the "conflict resolution mindset"

By listening to understand and getting creative, together we come up with a resolution that meets both my needs and the other person's needs.

Then take these four steps:

1. **Ask about the other person's need.**

2. **Explain your own need.**

3. **Brainstorm win-win solutions to meet both needs.**

4. **Jointly identify which options are acceptable to both of you.**

Step 1: Ask about the other person's need.

It's important for both parties to understand the difference between a want and a need. Wants are ways to satisfy needs. There may be many ways to satisfy a need, not just the way you and the other person initially want. So why does the other person want what they say they want? What *need* does this fulfill? Ask and then listen carefully to understand what they say, checking to make sure.

Here's a situation in which a team of trainers has to deliver a program to 47 sites in 10 states. The program lays out a next-generation approach to customer service. Natalie, a top executive, was concerned that the trainers were still too close to the first draft and tasked a new product developer to attempt an upgrade. After finishing the project, the developer discovers that the trainers are resistant to adopting the upgraded version.

Head trainer: "We don't like this new version. Everybody has learned the current version, and we're going with it."

Developer: "That version is like a rough draft. Natalie said it needed more work. You can't put that in front of people."

Head trainer: "The team prefers what we've got. We worked hard on it, and there's nothing wrong with it."

Developer: "So you're willing to go with the draft because you don't want to make the effort to adopt the polished version?"

Head trainer: "Look, there's no need. Nobody has any problems with it."

Developer: "Well, now we have an improved version. Why is it so important to go with the draft, instead?"

Head trainer: "I told you. Everyone on the team put a lot of work into getting ready to use the program as it is, and they see it as their program now. And nobody wants to go through that again."

Step 2: Explain your own need.

Remember that your initial demand isn't your need. It's just one way to satisfy your need. State your need, and then check to be sure you were understood. In this case, the developer and the head trainer seem to be at an impasse.

Developer: "I think I understand. At this point they feel the current version is their product. And the revision is my product. I get it."

Head trainer: "Good."

Developer: "But can I explain why I think it's important to put a revised program in front of the district offices?"

Head trainer: "Okay."

Developer: "As Natalie explained it to me, she's afraid the districts will find ways to criticize it and reject it. That's why she wanted me to go through it and kick it up a notch. And to be honest, lots of things needed work."

Head trainer: "Maybe so. But my team members are the ones who have to deliver it, and I know for a fact you're going to get resistance from them."

Step 3. Brainstorm win-win solutions to meet both needs.

Without further discussion, critique or justification, encourage the person to brainstorm with you to create a list of new options that will satisfy *both your need and their need* at the same time.

Developer: "I appreciate that. They haven't bought in. At the same time, it would be good for the whole company if this were well-received in the field. I'd like to explore ways to meet the needs of your team while at the same time putting out the best product, one they buy into."

Head trainer: "What do you have in mind?"

Developer: "Let's you and I get a little creative and come up with some possible ways to meet their needs and Natalie's need for a polished version. Okay?"

Head trainer: "All right. Do you have any ideas?"

Developer: "What if Natalie promises a special bonus if the districts give rave reviews?"

Head trainer: "That would be nice, but probably too expensive."

Developer: "It's just an idea. Let's do this without offering judgments at this point. Your turn. What's your suggestion for meeting both our needs?"

Head trainer: "I can't think of anything."

Developer: "Hey, I've seen you get creative. Give us an idea."

Head trainer: "Okay. How about this. We go with the current version, but if we get pushback, we regroup and go with the revision."

Developer: "That gives me another idea. What if Natalie puts the new version on the table and says it's an improvement but not great? And she tasks them to identify areas that still need work, and we all tweak it together."

Step 4. Jointly identify which options are acceptable to both of you.

Discuss the pros and cons of the creative options and select the one most acceptable to both of you.

Head trainer: "You know, that's pretty interesting. It would make a difference if they saw this as Natalie's thing and not your thing. And if they do the tweaking, they might well buy in."

Developer: "And the end product would be even better, and they would get the credit."

Head trainer: "You know what? I think this might work. Can you get Natalie to do her part?"

Developer: "I'm sure she'll be happy to do what's needed. She was serious that it needed improvement. Give me until tomorrow and let's talk."

In this scenario, the top executive wanted a better version and could have pushed it through. But the developer didn't have to play this power card. He didn't compete to win. And he didn't bargain or compromise. Natalie brought the revised version to the training team and told them it still wasn't good enough and asked them to make it right. And the team agreed. Both the developer and the trainers got what they needed, just not the way they initially thought.

Tips for optimizing the way you resolve conflict:

- **Self-regulate.** When you have the feeling of wanting to get your own way, that's your signal to shift into conflict resolution mode. If you cringe when you learn what the other person wants, keep these feelings to yourself. Instead, exercise patience, consideration and tact in order to listen to discover the person's wants and needs.

- **Get creative.** Rather than automatically standing your ground and getting involved in a power struggle, be open to alternate solutions. Put what both sides want aside and focus on what they need. Take the brainstorm approach: explore ways of meeting your needs as well as the needs of the other person.

- **Take the lead.** When you realize the person wants something you can't live with, recognize that you'll have to be the one to initiate the four steps of win-win creative conflict resolution.

- **Ask for cooperation.** Encourage the other person to listen and be creative while searching for solutions.

- **Practice with friends and family.** Conflicts are common, even between loving spouses. Take the lead to try the win-win approach to finding a solution that will work for both. Good practice!

- **Use the steps to facilitate conflict resolution between other people.** Don't expect them to be able to use this approach without your help. You can walk them through it, step by step, getting them to be creative about meeting their needs, rather than insisting on their initial demands.

Does the win-win approach really work? While it's true that some conflicts don't lend themselves to this method, most do. Denny once used the technique to help two executives who had been at odds and held grudges against each other for fifteen years. In the end, they shook hands and hugged each other. It's rare to find a situation in which the two initial wants are the only alternatives to a resolution.

Imagine the resentment you'll create if you simply lay down the law without making an effort to satisfy a person's needs. When both parties win, you invest in relationships.

To get your "reps," stay alert for conflict resolution moments, such as when someone wants something:

- You don't want them to do
- That's not supported by the budget
- That customers may not like
- That's not an urgent priority
- That violates policy
- That puts people or the organization at risk

This chapter in a nutshell:

- **Conflict resolution is not about winning the conflict. It's about finding a way to satisfy both people's needs.**

- **Listen to find out what the person wants, and then ask them about their needs—what their want will do for them.**

- **Explain your need, and then brainstorm alternative ways to satisfy both needs.**

Learn more about conflict resolution:

- Thomas Gordon, *Leader Effectiveness Training* (Tarcher-Perigee, 2001), Chapters 8, 9 and 10

- Roger Fisher, William Ury and Bruce Patton, *Getting to Yes* (Penguin, 2011)

- Dudley Weeks, *The Eight Essential Steps to Conflict Resolution* (Tarcher-Putnam, 1992)

- Mel Silberman, *PeopleSmart* (Barrett-Koehler, 2000), Skill 6

- Stephen R. Covey, *The 7 Habits of Highly Effective People,* Revised Ed. (Free Press, 2004), Habit 4

PART THREE

....

The Path to Mastery

This book focuses on what we consider the top 10 communication skills. Its goal is to help you replace dysfunctional behavior patterns with mutually beneficial ones. By now you appreciate that making this effort is a significant undertaking. As Mark Twain said, "Habit is habit and not to be flung out of the window by any man, but coaxed downstairs one step at a time."

We recommend that you work on all 10 skills—one at a time, keeping in mind that mastery is a relative term. Even if you make dramatic progress at first, you can continue to improve a skill throughout your life.

Success is definitely within your reach, if you make a long-term commitment. To stick with it, keep the many payoffs in mind.

"We resist new maneuvers because they make us feel clumsy, awkward and more at risk. But if you want to accelerate your rate of achievement rapidly, you must search out and vigorously employ new behaviors."

Price Pritchett

"Few things are impossible to diligence and skill. Great works are performed not by strength, but perseverance."

Samuel Johnson

14

....

How You Can Continuously Improve Over Time

We wrote this book to help you strengthen your workplace relationships. We've focused only on this handful of skills because we believe they have the most beneficial impact for people in the workplace. It would be daunting to attempt more. If you tried to improve many people skills all at once, you'd soon be overwhelmed.

It's going to be challenging enough to work on these 10 skills. As we affirmed in Chapter 3 ("The Secret to Improving Communication Skills"), you're unlikely to use any of them in the heat of the moment on a busy, tiring day if you haven't established the skills as your dominant pattern—an automatic, comfortable habit. And the brain cells involved in the skill won't connect into an empowering circuit for a new habit from just one successful experience. While each repetition will stimulate the brain cells to wire together and insulate, it will take many reps to finish the job. Every artisan knows this. Every athlete knows this. Anyone who has ever tried to change a habit or master a skill knows this. And this journey could be frustrating, because old habits will sometimes kick in before you've wired your brain for the new, more effective habits. Learning from your successes and lapses will take time and persistence. You'll need to stay committed.

Now that you've read the chapters of Part Two and have familiarized yourself with the skills, you may be thinking, *What should I do now? What's the best way to start improving the way I connect with my coworkers?* The purpose of this chapter is to answer this question and get you started on your learning journey. In these final pages, we outline a plan we believe will work to make you a better communicator.

Become more empathetic with people.

Working on interpersonal skills requires a long-term commitment. Consider how hard it would be to stay the course if you didn't care about the people around you, if you weren't genuinely interested in who they are—their lives, their challenges, and their ambitions.

As you continue developing your sense of compassion, whenever you encounter another person, try to imagine what their personal experience is right at that moment: their perceptions, thoughts, feelings, values, attitudes, goals, and imaginings. Everyone is different. Make it your goal to learn about these differences. Your ability to genuinely appreciate people will have a positive impact on how you apply the skills.

Practice recognizing your reactive moments.

In the past, you may have had a surge of frustration or anger that led to raising your voice, or worse: toxic questions, put-downs, sarcasm, name-calling, threats, ultimatums, commands, lectures, and so on. If so, you may have felt a twinge of remorse afterward, because you know that reactions like these will not, in the end, help you build positive, cooperative relationships. In the moment when you "lost your cool," you were probably too upset to be aware that you were "reacting" instead of communicating effectively.

We suggest that before you make a serious project of working on any of the skills, do two things:

- Practice *being self-aware* in those moments when you feel your emotions rising, when you feel the urge to lash out or play the authority card.

- Instead of expressing yourself emotionally, take a deep breath and say or do nothing. Just walk away until you feel calm again.

Doing this a few times will help you build a pattern of self-control, which will set you up for exercising a skill instead.

Focus on improving one skill at a time.

Doing the work to get good at *one* of the 10 skills is all most busy people can handle. Like multi-tasking, the failure to focus would be counter-productive. Our advice is to work on one skill, with its subskills and tips for refinement, until you feel so comfortable with it that it becomes your automatic, go-to response. Only then will you get consistent results while trying to improve another skill.

It's also a good idea to focus on one element of the skill at a time. For example, when learning to be a better listener, spend time improving the way you sense the other person and express empathy, one of the important elements of listening.

Likewise, once you've become comfortable with the skill, aim for refining your effectiveness. Each chapter suggests "tips," which you can consciously focus on—one at a time—when practicing the skill and learning from these experiences.

Work on becoming a better listener first.

We recommended this approach in Chapter 4 ("Listen to Understand"). Listening is an essential component of each of the other skills. For example, when trying to resolve a conflict, your coworker will try to give reasons for what they want to do; to discover their core need, you'll need to understand their reasons.

The payoff for being a good listener is huge. Relationships are a two-way street. Both you and the people around you have to make an effort to connect. When others sense that they're being heard, they'll feel understood and valued. Making an effort to truly understand what they're trying to say is a gesture of respect, something every person wants and will appreciate. If they sense you're really listening, they'll conclude the effort to open up to you is worth it. More than any other skill, listening to understand will help nurture the relationship between you and everyone you encounter at work.

Make a priority of learning to recognize when to use a skill.

One of the most frustrating aspects of learning a communication skill is realizing that you've missed an opportunity to use it. In the previous chapters we stressed these opportunities, such as "the listening moment" and "the feedback moment." To help you spot them during the flow of your busy life, the descriptions of these moments are summarized in Appendix 2 ("Summary of 'Communication Moments' and 'Communication Mindsets'").

The same recommendation applies to engaging the ideal mindset for each of the skills. Studying them will help you fix these attitudes in your mind.

Practice putting the steps/subskills together in a continuous flow.

While it's an effective learning technique to focus on one step/subskill at a time, your ultimate goal is to get comfortable using all the elements. Some of the skills, such as conflict resolution, work best when you apply the steps in sequence. But in real life, your interaction may not follow that order. Your coworker may skip a step or jump to the desired end result without your help, which is fine. Or you may achieve the connection you hope for using just one aspect of a skill, such as restating expectations when giving feedback. You approach mastery when you have the confidence to go with the flow of the interaction instead of following a procedure lock-step, which might feel awkward and unnatural to both of you at first.

Practice with everyone.

The focus of this book is to help you cultivate the connection you have with the people you encounter at work. These are the same skills used by professionals such as mediators, therapists and counselors, who depend on effective communication in their practice. You can achieve wonderful benefits by using them with your spouse, other family members, and friends. In all these relationships, there are countless moments for connecting well. For example, when you express empathy with your child, the experience helps ingrain the skill for expressing it with team members. When you use the skills to resolve a conflict with your manager, you'll find it easier to do the same thing with your spouse.

Learn from your mistakes.

When you forget what you could have done or your best effort doesn't go well, ask yourself:

"What happened? What did I say? How do I feel about it?"

"Why did I say it that way?"

"What effect did this have on the other person?"

"What can I do next time to get better results?"

"What's my next step?"

Ask for coaching.

The great thing about having a coach is that they hold you accountable, give you feedback, and encourage you. Of course, not every employee can invest in working one-on-one with a professional coach. This isn't what we're suggesting. We designed this book to be a coaching resource, and we hope you use it to stay on track with the best practices while encouraging yourself to keep trying.

But a book can't replace a caring individual who can, for example, offer feedback. If you have a willing manager, a trusted colleague, or a friend who is also dealing with relationships at work, you can spend time sharing stories and frustrations. But instead of giving advice, you can coach each other. You can "listen to understand" and "coach each other to think" about problems and solutions. You can encourage them to read this book so you can work on the skills together, holding each other accountable, giving feedback, helping each other learn from experience, and encouraging each other.

Be patient.

Interpersonal skills are complex, and you have to fight through the tendency to fall back on old, comfortable habits. Even if you follow our recommendation to work on one skill at a time, getting comfortable with that one skill could take weeks, even months. Skill-building isn't an event; it's a process that requires real-world application, recovering from mistakes, and learning from successes and setbacks—a long series of experiences that slowly cause the brain cells involved in the skill to wire into a circuit and then insulate with myelin. There's no magic bullet or miracle cure, unless you consider "doing the work" the secret sauce. Millions of people have become comfortable with new skills because they persisted in spite of lapses and mistakes.

You'll be successful, you'll feel your relationships with others growing stronger, if you *don't give up.*

When people disappoint you or frustrate you, recognize your rising emotions. And instead of reacting, just breathe. Calm yourself, forgive them, and forgive yourself. Think about which of the skills you can use in the moment, and do your best. If it doesn't go as well as you hoped, review the appropriate chapter in Part Two and learn from what happened. Remember your goal, why you're trying to be a better communicator: to preserve and nurture the bond you have with the people around you. Stay committed for the long haul.

Keep trying.

This chapter in a nutshell:

- **Learn to recognize moments when a certain skill will help you.**
- **Work on one skill at a time.**
- **Get good at listening first.**
- **Practice the communication skills with everyone in your life, not just coworkers.**
- **Learn from your mistakes. Improving a skill is a journey involving successes and shortfalls.**
- **Work past discouragement. Don't give up.**

Learn more about creating new work habits:

- James Clear, *Atomic Habits* (Avery-Penguin, 2018)
- Charles Duhigg, *The Power of Habit* (Random House, 2012)
- Robin Sharma, *The 5 AM Club* (HarperCollins, 2018)

- Amy Johnson, *The Little Book of Big Change* (New Harbinger, 2016)

"To be able to communicate effectively...one-to-one goes far toward determining your own success in life."

Norman Vincent Peale

15

....

Your Impact

In Chapter 3 ("The Secret to Improving Communication Skills"), Chapter 14 ("How You Can Continuously Improve Over Time"), and in each of the skill-building chapters in between, we trust that two things have become clear:

- These skills have powerful benefits.

- Shifting from old habits to these improved skills requires a long-term effort.

Attending a seminar or a three-day course can be a wonderful introduction, but rewiring the part of your brain that drives these skills will happen only if you apply what you learn for weeks or months—one skill at a time.

This means that improving the skills related to being a strong leader or an influential, high-performing team member needs to be an aspect of lifelong learning. It also means that your efforts to improve are based on your desire to really connect with people—to overcome the inherent separateness between human beings. With empathy, you can begin to learn more about the people around you, what they know, what they're capable of, and what motivates them.

The payoff can be amazing.

When you communicate in a way that expresses genuine caring, the people around you will respect you, believe in you, and trust you to be there for them.

When you listen deeply, it demonstrates that you care about the person and what they're trying to say. When you make a habit of asking for their ideas and opinions, it not only stimulates them to become better problem solvers, it's seen as a sign of respect. When you give feedback that encourages, they know you're looking out for their best interests, as well as team results. When you accept feedback graciously, people will feel it's safe to tell you things you need to know, instead of withholding these insights out of fear that you'll react negatively. When you engage in dialogue and try to resolve conflicts creatively, you'll move the enterprise forward instead of stirring up ill will.

Team members will be inspired to elevate their level of effort, producing better results.

People have unique strengths and talents, and it's astonishing what they can do *if they want to* and work as a team. But if they distrust their leaders and coworkers, they'll fear their best efforts will go unappreciated or they'll be taken advantage of. When you apply empowering communication skills, you'll naturally bring out their best. And good things can happen:

- You'll become a stronger leader. As a result, your team's efforts will be noticed and managers will want to find ways for you to contribute at a higher level.

- As you and your coworkers achieve results, everyone's confidence and feelings of self-worth will be strengthened.

- Along with your ability to lead, you'll become a better coach to the people around you, helping them grow stronger as contributors.

The positive ways you relate to others will affect the way they behave with each other.

When team members receive coaching from their managers and peers, they'll notice and try applying the skills with each other, enabling them to support each other to learn and develop. As team members do this, they'll be fostering a more engaged and energized workforce. This is known as a "coaching culture," where leaders and team contributors alike:

- Demonstrate curiosity and listen to each other with an open mind

- Ask questions that help another person solve a problem or analyze a mistake

- Help each other improve their performance

- Feel safe being honest with each other, providing both appreciation and constructive feedback as needed

- Look for ways to support their manager, coworkers and others

- Resolve issues more quickly, so they have more time to be productive

- Do the hard things necessary to achieve an ambitious goal or work through a difficult situation

The communication skills that enrich work relationships are the same skills that enrich personal relationships.

The skills involved in listening to coworkers work wonderfully when listening to friends and family. The kind of affirming and constructive feedback that encourages coworkers is the best way to give feedback to anyone. The approach to dialogue and resolving conflicts recommended in this book is the classic way to avoid arguments and power struggles in any relationship. Becoming a more supportive, caring coworker can make you a better spouse, a better parent, and a better friend.

It all starts with someone like you who cares about people and who wants to connect more effectively. It's a process of self-development that never ends, and along the way everyone will be inspired by the way you lead and coach, regardless of your role in the organization.

This chapter in a nutshell:

- **Communicating effectively to build relationships will inspire people to perform at their best.**

- **The elevated performance of the people around you will make you successful.**

- **As your coworkers pick up the skills you're modeling, they'll learn to coach each other. This dynamic is what is known as a "coaching culture."**

- **A huge bonus: workplace communication skills work wonderfully well in personal relationships.**

Learn more about a compassionate approach to workplace relationships:

- Monica Worline and Jane Dutton, *Awakening Compassion at Work* (Barret-Koehler, 2017)

- Christopher Kukk, *The Compassionate Achiever* (Harper-Collins, 2017)

- Stephen R. Covey, *The 7 Habits of Highly Effective People,* Revised Ed. (Free Press, 2004), Habits 5 and 6

- Michael J. Gelb, *The Art of Connection* (New World Library, 2017)

Support Tools for You

For over 30 years, our software company has focused on creating technologies that address the 10 communications skills described in this book, along with many other skills. If you'd like to expand your assessment and development resources, one of our tools may be the perfect complement.

ASSESSMENT:
This 360/survey software makes it a snap to gather performance feedback so your development resources are focused on the greatest areas of need. You can start with a baseline survey, survey again later, and then compare the two results to measure performance improvements.

Customize each survey and use a single tool for all these applications:

- Pre-training assessment to identify skills to address
- Performance improvement (pre- and post-training)
- Leader and team contributor development
- Team and organization-wide feedback

DEVELOPMENT:
Learning events like classroom or online training can be excellent introductions to new skills, but they're not enough to establish habits for workplace performance. This online technology provides post-training follow-up. It gives participants the structure, practice and support they need to take skills from

awkward to *automatic.* Each subscription includes an electronic copy of this book.

Ways you can use this tool:

- As a component of a training class

- Post-training follow-up

- Stand-alone tool for learning and development

- Technology support for peer coaching

- Remote learning

Learn more at:
https://GrowStrongLeaders.com

Appendix 1

Summary of Suggested Reading

For readers who want to learn more about skill-building and interpersonal communication, here are some books that have influenced our thinking.

Beard, Colin and John P. Wilson. *Experiential Learning*, 4th Ed. (Kogan Page, 2018).

Bell, Meredith. *Strong for Performance* (First Summit Publishing, 2020).

Blanchard, Ken and Spencer Johnson. *The New One Minute Manager* (William Morrow, 2015).

Clear, James. *Atomic Habits* (Avery-Penguin, 2018).

Covey, Stephen R. *The 7 Habits of Highly Effective People,* Revised Ed. (Free Press, 2004).

Crabb, Larry. *Encouragement: The Unexpected Power of Building Others Up* (Zondervan, 2013).

Crane, Thomas G. *The Heart of Coaching*, 4th Ed. (FTA Press, 2014).

Djukich, Dusan. *Straight-Line Leadership* (Robert D. Reed, 2011).

Duhigg, Charles. *The Power of Habit* (Random House, 2012).

Fisher, Roger, with William Ury and Bruce Patton. *Getting to Yes* (Penguin, 2011).

Folkman, Joe. *Turning Feedback into Change* (Novations, 1996).

Gelb, Michael J. *The Art of Connection* (New World Library, 2017).

Goldsmith, Marshall. *What Got You Here Won't Get You There* (Hyperion, 2007).

Gordon, Thomas. *Leader Effectiveness Training* (TarcherPerigee, 2001).

Goulston, Mark. *Just Listen* (AMACOM, 2015).

Hardy, Benjamin. *Willpower Doesn't Work* (Hatchett Books, 2018).

Isaacs, William. *Dialogue* (Random House, 2008).

Johnson, Amy. *The Little Book of Big Change* (New Harbinger, 2016).

Kaner, Sam. *Facilitator's Guide to Participatory Decision-Making* (Jossey-Bass, 2014).

Kaufman, Josh. *The First 20 Hours* (Penguin, 2013).

Kukk, Christopher. *The Compassionate Achiever* (HarperCollins, 2017).

Lerner, Harriet. *Why Won't You Apologize?: Healing Big Betrayals and Everyday Hurts* (Gallery Books, 2017).

Marchand, Marie-Eve. *The Spirit of Dialogue in a Digital Age* (Dialogue Publications, 2019).

Maurer, Rick. *Feedback Toolkit* (Productivity Press, 1994).

Maurer, Robert. *One Small Step Can Change Your Life* (Workman, 2014).

Maxwell, John C. *Developing the Leader within You* (HarperCollins, 2019).

Maxwell, John C. *The 21 Irrefutable Laws of Leadership* (Thomas Nelson, 2007).

Rock, David. *Quiet Leadership* (HarperBusiness, 2007).

Rock, David and Linda Page. *Coaching with the Brain in Mind* (Wiley, 2009).

Sharma, Robin. *The Leader Who Had No Title* (Free Press, 2010).

Sharma, Robin. *The 5 AM Club* (HarperCollins, 2018).

Silberman, Mel. *PeopleSmart* (Barrett-Koehler, 2000).

Stanier, Michael Bungay. *The Coaching Habit* (Box of Crayons Press, 2016).

Weeks, Dudley. *The Eight Essential Steps to Conflict Resolution* (Tarcher-Putnam, 1992).

Worline, Monica and Jane Dutton. *Awakening Compassion at Work* (Barret-Koehler, 2017).

Appendix 2

Summary of "Communication Moments" and "Communication Mindsets"

In order to apply communication skills effectively, it's important to first recognize opportunities to use them and engage the right attitude.

Listen to Understand
(Chapter 4)

The "listening moment"

...when someone is trying to tell you something you need to hear.

The "listening mindset"

I care about this person's problems, thoughts, and feelings. Something is going on with them right now, and I want to know what it is. So rather than react negatively or assume I understand, I check what I'm hearing.

Coach People to Think for Themselves (Chapter 5)

The "thinking moment"

...when you can encourage someone to do their own thinking, rather than giving them the answer or solution.

The "thinking mindset"

I ask open-ended questions that encourage my team members to practice thinking: understanding, reasoning, evaluating, problem-solving, decision-making, goal-setting, planning, and organizing.

Guide Learning from Experience (Chapter 6)

The "learning moment"

...when something significant has happened, and your coworker can learn from it.

The "learning mindset"

I ask open-ended questions that encourage my team members to analyze what happened so they can improve the way they approach their work in the future.

Get Buy-in for Expectations
(Chapter 7)

The "buy-in moment"

...when faced with a goal, milestone or task, and you expect specific effort or results from a coworker.

The "buy-in mindset"

People are more motivated to accomplish a difficult objective if they own it, and so I ask for their input to help frame it.

Offer Encouragement
(Chapter 8)

The "encouragement moment"

...when you notice that something has happened to cause a coworker to be discouraged.

The "encouragement mindset"

People sometimes don't bounce back from adversity right away. I remind them of their strengths, what's possible, and that their coworkers want to support them.

Express Appreciation
(Chapter 9)

The "appreciation moment"

...when you notice that someone has done something well, made a special effort, or achieved something outstanding.

The "appreciation mindset"

I notice when people have done their best and affirm them for their effort.

Give Feedback Constructively
(Chapter 10)

The "feedback moment"

...when a coworker's performance has come up short and you want to inspire them to do better.

The "feedback mindset"

When I'm not happy with someone's behavior, I share how I feel about it in a positive, encouraging way.

Accept Feedback Graciously
(Chapter 11)

The "accept feedback graciously moment"

...when someone has given you feedback and you want to encourage this kind of input in the future.

The "accept feedback graciously mindset"

I ask for feedback, and when someone gifts me with it in any form, I listen without reacting, thank them, and follow up with an effort to change my behavior.

Engage in Dialogue
(Chapter 12)

The "dialogue moment"

...when you realize that you don't agree with someone's point of view.

The "dialogue mindset"

I may disagree with someone, but we're entitled to our opinions. Without trying to win an argument, I keep an open mind and make an effort to learn why the other person has this opinion.

Resolve Conflict Creatively
(Chapter 13)

The "conflict resolution moment"

...when someone wants something you consider unacceptable or you want something another person considers unacceptable.

The "conflict resolution mindset"

By listening to understand and getting creative, together we come up with a resolution that meets both my needs and the other person's needs.

Appendix 3

The 5 Magic Reflection Questions

Learning from experience is about on-the-job learning: quickly making a conscious effort to mine what has happened at work and discovering the lessons that lead to improvement. You do this by asking these open-ended questions:

1. **What happened?** The details of an event need to be recalled in order to make sense of them. What was the sequence of events? What did you do? How did others react? How do you feel about it?

2. **Why did you handle it this way?** Things happen for a reason. To imagine a better way to handle a situation like this, try to understand why things occurred the way they did. What were you thinking? What helped or hindered? What led to the outcome?

3. **What were the consequences?** Appreciating the impact of what happened creates the motivation to handle situations like this more effectively. Benefits? Costs? Problems? Resolutions?

4. **How would you handle a similar situation in the future?** What did you learn from this experience? What basic principles? How are you going to apply the lesson?

5. **What are your next steps?** What will you do in the next 48 hours to set you up for implementing this learning?

Appendix 4
Core Strengths

One of the benefits of working on challenging projects is that they can make your team members stronger as individuals. These are opportunities to exercise the personal behavior patterns that lead to success. You can encourage people when the going gets tough, give them feedback, listen to them, and help them learn from their experiences.

To help you appreciate the behavior patterns they could be forming, here's a list of core strengths team members can build.

Personal Growth
1. Self-development
2. Self-awareness
3. Self-esteem
4. Self-confidence
5. Perseverance
6. Optimism
7. Acceptance
8. Courage
9. Gratitude
10. Self-discipline

Performance/Work Ethic
1. Initiative
2. Patience
3. Passion
4. Creativity
5. Focus
6. Commitment
7. Effort
8. Excellence
9. Thoroughness
10. Accountability

Relationships
1. Fairness
2. Loyalty
3. Tolerance
4. Trust
5. Cooperation
6. Compassion
7. Honesty
8. Integrity
9. Open-mindedness
10. Service

Leadership
1. Awareness
2. Responsibility
3. Empowerment
4. Decisiveness
5. Vision
6. Flexibility
7. Proactivity
8. Rationality
9. Intuition
10. Composure

Acknowledgements

We've been creating assessment and development tools for workplace relationship-building skills for more than 30 years. Along the way, we've had stimulating input from colleagues who've affirmed and challenged us, always leading to better thinking and outcomes.

A special thanks to Dr. Mark Goulston, whose book *Just Listen* is the absolute best on this foundational skill. Mark has been an incredibly valuable mentor whose concern for others comes through clearly in everything he says or writes.

These colleagues have been devoted users and resellers of our products for decades, providing us with valuable ideas and suggestions that have been incorporated into our products: Rick and Susan Stamm, Bud Cummings, Mark Spool, Graham Da Costa, Mark Hinderliter, Elizabeth Fried, Dennis LaMountain, Camille Harris, Janyne Peek Emsick, Larry Brower, Alice Dendinger and Nick Scalzo.

As with previous books, we're indebted to Kathleen Scott for her careful reading, editing and unwavering support.

Our supremely talented editor at First Summit Publishing, Paula Schlauch, has also been our business partner for almost 30 years. Paula not only managed every detail of this book's production, she also shared a spirit of love, generosity and calmness that helped us finish this project with focus and joy. We are grateful for her steadfast presence and unwavering commitment.

About the Authors

As CEO of Performance Support Systems, Dr. Coates has published articles, books, and online programs for workplace communication skills for over 30 years. These award-winning, brain-based assessment and learning programs have been used by millions of people worldwide. A graduate of West Point (1967), he retired from the U.S. Army as a lieutenant colonel (1987). He earned his Ph.D. from Duke University (1977) and has served on the faculties of the United States Military Academy, the Armed Forces Staff College, the College of William and Mary, and the Center for Creative Leadership.

An entrepreneur since 1982, Meredith Bell has been an expert in helping companies develop the people side of their business. As President and co-founder of Performance Support Systems, a global software company, she has worked with thousands of business leaders, human resource professionals, talent and learning executives, entrepreneurs, consultants, and coaches. Meredith is the host of the popular Grow Strong Leaders Podcast and is also a frequent guest on podcasts, where she addresses topics such as communications skills for the workplace, the benefits of a focus on giving and being of service, and what's required to develop positive habits and skills over time.

Denny and Meredith have created award-winning brain-based learning and development programs for leaders and teams. They are available as podcast guests and as speakers at corporate or association events.

Quantity sales. Special discounts are available on quantity purchases by corporations, associations and others.

Contact us:

info@GrowStrongLeaders.com
757-656-4765
https://GrowStrongLeaders.com

Made in the USA
Middletown, DE
15 June 2022

66950597R00126